Children, Culture, and Controversy

Children, Culture, and Controversy

Mark I. West

Archon Books 1988

First published 1988 as an Archon Book,
an imprint of The Shoe String Press, Inc.,
Hamden, Connecticut 06514

Printed in the United States of America

The paper used in this publication meets the
minimum requirements of
American National Standard for Information Sciences-
Permanence of Paper for Printed Library Materials,
ANSI 239.48–1984. ∞

Library of Congress Cataloging-in-Publication Data
West, Mark I.
    Children, culture, and controversy / Mark I. West.
        p. cm.
    Bibliography: p.
    Includes index.
    ISBN 0-208-02155-8 (alk. paper)
    1. Children—United States—Social conditions.   2. United
States—Popular culture.   3. Child rearing—United States.
    4. Moral development—United States.   5. Censorship—
United   States.   6. Innocence (Psychology)   I. Title.
    HQ792.U5W43 1988   88-14760
    305.2′3—dc19   CIP

For Larry Friedman,
my friend and mentor

Contents

Acknowledgments

Over the course of writing this book, I drew on the advice, expertise and support of many people. The person who helped me the most is Lawrence Friedman of Bowling Green State University. He encouraged me to begin the book, read and critiqued many of the chapters, and prodded me to complete the book when I found myself drifting toward other projects. Several other people provided helpful critiques of some of the chapters, including Arthur Neal, Gary Hess, Donald Enholm, the late Frank Baldanza, and the late Paul Pruyser.

A number of people helped with particular chapters. Malinda Lee, Ann Wicker and John Grooms all contributed to chapter seven. Chapter eight benefited greatly from the cooperation of Judy Blume and Norma Klein, and chapter nine is much stronger because of the help I received from Timothy Dyk.

I received research grants from the Children's Literature Association, the Foundation of the University of North Carolina at Charlotte and the State of North Carolina, and I appreciate this assistance.

I also wish to thank Ann Wilson, Judy Lassiter, and especially Juanita Honeycutt for preparing the final manuscript, and Steve Matthews for his encouragement.

Finally, I want to express my gratitude to my wife, Nancy

Acknowledgments

Northcott. Although she entered my life when this book was already underway, she quickly took a strong interest in it and soon became my chief consultant. She still holds this position even though the book is finally finished.

1.

The Idea of Childhood Innocence and Its Impact on Children's Culture

Most dictionaries define childhood as the time between birth and puberty, but this definition ignores the word's many connotations. As it is generally used, childhood is much more than an age span; it is a set of ideas. Some of these ideas stem from religious beliefs, and some grow out of political or economic developments. Still others reflect cultural movements or scientific research. From time to time, ideas associated with childhood fall out of favor and new ideas may take their place. Thus, the history of childhood is really a history of ideas.

Although the entire American adult population has never embraced a unified set of ideas about childhood, certain ideas have predominated during particular time periods, which children's books and other forms of children's culture have tended to reflect. Whenever a dominant set of ideas about childhood has been challenged or replaced, the characteristics of American children's culture have changed accordingly. In the mid-1700s, the first such change occurred.

In a landmark study of adult ideas about childhood during America's colonial period, historian Philip Greven found that not all colonists viewed children in the same light. Most colonial parents, Greven argued, belonged to one of three groups: the "evangelicals," the "genteel," and the "moderates." The adults whom Greven classified as evangelicals generally believed in the tenets of orthodox Calvinism. The genteel, according to Greven's classification system, consisted of the members of America's emerging gentry. Greven's third group, the moderates, shared many of the religious values of the evangelicals, but they disagreed with the Calvinist notion of infant depravity. Each of these groups had its own child-rearing beliefs and practices.

Especially in New England, the child-rearing philosophy of Greven's evangelicals dominated the approaches of other colonial parents during the 1600s and early 1700s. The evangelicals believed that all people, including newborn infants, are innately sinful, and their child-rearing techniques were designed to instill this belief in children.[1] The books that evangelical parents provided for their children also reflected this belief. Even the rhyming alphabet contained in the *New England Primer*, the most famous of these books, was predicated upon the idea of infant depravity:

> In Adam's fall
> We sinned all.
>
> Thy life to mend
> God's Book attend.[2]

Similar theological moralizing was communicated to the children of evangelicals through such works as James Janeway's *A Token for Children* and John Cotton's *Milk for Babes*.[3]

As the eighteenth century progressed, the evangelicals' approach to child-rearing gradually began to decline in popularity. The genteel, according to Greven, completely rejected the Calvinist conception of childhood. Rather than think of children as sinners, genteel parents tended to view children as precious beings who deserved to be indulged and pampered.[4] The adults whom Greven classified as moderates felt that the genteel style of parenting spoiled children, and some moderates criticized genteel parents for neglecting the religious training of children.[5] On one important issue, however, genteel parents and moderates were in complete agreement; both groups believed that infants are innocent of sin.

For the genteel and the moderates, John Locke replaced Calvin as the most trusted authority on matters pertaining to

2

child-rearing. Locke's *Essay Concerning Human Understanding* and *Some Thoughts Concerning Education* were readily available in eighteenth-century America, and the child-rearing advice that these works contained was widely followed by both genteel and moderate parents. Locke did not believe in the existence of innate ideas or in the doctrine of infant depravity. Claiming that the minds of infants are essentially blank, Locke argued that ideas and morality are determined by experience. His views on the nature of children's minds led Locke to disagree with the evangelicals' repressive methods of child-rearing. Since he did not believe in the doctrine of original sin, he saw no reason to make children feel guilt-ridden. Instead, he urged parents to teach morality by controlling their children's experiences, by setting good examples, and by developing their children's reasoning abilities.[6]

Locke's child-rearing philosophy had an important impact on the development of children's literature in both England and America. After studying Locke's educational theories, John Newbery, an English publisher and author, decided to publish books that provided children with the type of moral and intellectual instruction that Locke had recommended. Newbery's first children's book, *A Little Pretty Pocket-Book*, appeared in 1744, and many others soon followed. In all of these publications, Newbery attempted to teach children about morality, manners, history, spelling, and numerous other subjects "by way of diversion."[7] In the 1750s, copies of Newbery's books made their way across the Atlantic and were purchased by American parents and teachers.

With the outbreak of the American Revolution, the amount of English goods that reached American shores declined sharply. Among the goods that Americans no longer had easy access to were Newbery's books. Soon after the revolution came to a close, Isaiah Thomas, an enterprising printer from Worcester, Massachusetts, felt that there might be a market for American editions of Newbery's publications. In 1784, he pirated a primer by Newbery, and by 1790 he was publishing practically every book from Newbery's stock.[8] Soon publishers from other cities in the United States began following Thomas's example. These publishers, however, often made changes in Newbery's books in order to make them more suitable for American tastes. For

3

example, since religious fervency was somewhat stronger in America than in England, the American publishers replaced the riddles and jokes in Newbery's books with hymns and prayers.[9]

During the early decades of the nineteenth century, the attitudes of a number of influential adults toward children began to change. Several American intellectuals from this period rejected the Lockean notion that children begin life as blank tablets and adopted, instead, a belief that children are naturally good. This development was tied to the rise of romanticism and its sentimental view of childhood. Such romantic works as William Blake's *Songs of Innocence*, William Wordsworth's "Ode: Intimations of Immortality from Recollections of Early Childhood," and especially Jean Jacques Rousseau's *Emile* all had an impact on Americans' beliefs about childhood.[10] As the century progressed, an increasing number of articulate Americans found themselves in agreement with Rousseau's basic rule about child psychology:

> Let us lay down as an incontrovertible rule that the first impulses of nature are always right; there is no original sin in the human heart, and the how and why of the entrance of every vice can be traced.[11]

In the 1830s, proponents of the idea of childhood innocence started writing books on child-rearing. Bronson Alcott, one of the first authors to provide parents with a child-rearing manual that was not based on the concept of infant depravity, brought out *Observations on the Principles and Methods of Infant Instruction* in 1830. Alcott's book was soon followed by Lydia Maria Child's *The Mother's Book*, George Ackerley's *On the Management of Children in Sickness and Health*, Lyman Cobb's *The Evil Tendencies of Corporal Punishment*, Horace Bushnell's *Views of Christian Nurture*, and Elizabeth Blackwell's *The Moral Education of the Young*. Parents who read these books were told that they should attempt to preserve the natural innocence of children. The best way to accomplish this goal, the authors argued, was for parents to gently and gradually guide their children's moral development.[12]

Concern over the preservation of childhood innocence led some writers to pay particular attention to the cultural milieu that surrounded children. They argued that children's moral outlooks

4

are affected by the cultural forces with which they come into contact. One particularly optimistic author went so far as to argue that if these forces are properly controlled any child could be formed "into an angel."[13] Children's culture became a topic of considerable interest. Indeed, some writers argued that children's culture could be used to reinforce and refine the inborn goodness of children.

The emergence of American children's literature in the 1830s and '40s reflected the changing attitudes of adults toward children's entertainment. After becoming convinced that literature could be used to foster children's moral and intellectual growth, authors such as Samuel Goodrich and Jacob Abbott began writing and publishing didactic children's books. Through their books, these authors attempted both to entertain and instruct their readers.[14] Children's books from this period often included introductory comments intended for parents in which the authors discussed the value of children's literature. In *Rollo at Play*, for example, Abbott told parents that, in addition to entertaining children, his book was meant to cultivate "the thinking powers," promote "the progress of children in reading," and foster "the amiable and gentle qualities of the heart."[15]

Another development of children's culture during the second quarter of the nineteenth century was the appearance of children's magazines. *The Juvenile Miscellany*, founded by Lydia Maria Child, began publication in 1826, and the following year *Youth's Companion* appeared. The 1830s and '40s witnessed the birth of several other children's periodicals, including *Parley's Magazine*, *Robert Merry's Museum*, *Every Youth's Gazette*, *The Boys' and Girls' Magazine*, and *Fireside Companion*. Like children's books from this period, these magazines were meant to improve their readers.[16] The editors of *Youth's Companion* spoke for most other editors of children's magazines when they wrote that their objectives were "to inculcate truth by brief narratives, familiar illustrations, short biographies, and amusing anecdotes" and "to excite attention to good things by entertaining matter."[17]

At the same time that American children's books and magazines came into being, the board game made its American debut. In 1832, Anne W. Abbott, the daughter of a New England clergyman, came up with the idea of using a board game to teach children about such topics as honesty, humility, charity, and gratitude. She called her game *The Mansion of Happiness* and she convinced a printer in Salem, Massachusetts to manufacture and sell it.[18] Abbott prefaced her directions on how to play the game with a short poem in which she expressed sentiments similar to those voiced by the earlier authors of American children's literature:

> At this amusement each will find
> A moral to improve the mind:
> It gives to those their proper due,
> Who various paths of vice pursue,
> And shows (while vice destruction brings)
> That GOOD from every Virtue springs,
> Be virtuous then and forward press,
> To gain the seat of Happiness.[19]

By the second half of the nineteenth century, the reification of the notion of childhood innocence was well under way. References to infant depravity all but vanished from mid-nineteenth-century child-rearing manuals. Indeed, Jacob Abbott's *Gentle Measures in the Management and Training of the Young*, the most popular book on child-rearing published during this period, recommended that children never be told that they are sinners. Children's bad habits, Abbott argued, are the fault of parents, not children.[20] Some of Abbott's contemporaries suggested that industrialized society was the cause of children's faults. They argued that urban congestion, child labor, and inadequate schooling transformed otherwise innocent children into juvenile delinquents.[21] Images of children in much of the popular literature from the mid-nineteenth century, such as Charles Dickens's best-selling novels about virtuous waifs struggling to survive in crowded cities, lent support to these arguments.

A firm belief in the idea of childhood innocence led some authors and other creators of children's culture to conclude that much of the blatant moralizing that was so evident in children's books, magazines, and games from the 1830s, '40s, and '50s was unnecessary. They felt that the natural goodness of children meant that children's culture could afford to be more entertaining. Hence, the 1860s saw the publication of Thomas Bailey Aldrich's *The Story of a Bad Boy*, Louisa May Alcott's *Little Women*, and other children's books that contained only a moderate number of moralistic sermons.[22] Although the child characters in these books had minor faults, they generally continued to be cast in the mold of the innocent child.

After the Civil War, most forms of children's culture that adults purchased for children were predicated upon the idea of childhood innocence. Around the same time, however, some children themselves became direct consumers of children's culture. The books and other forms of culture that children selected on their own often dealt with violence and other topics that, according to the concept of childhood innocence, children were not supposed to find interesting. The popularity of these types of culture among children suggested that they were not as innocent as some adults wished them to be.

Although many people frowned upon the culture that youngsters selected on their own, a few reformers abhorred it and felt compelled to campaign against it. In the process of waging their campaigns, these reformers passionately, although not always logically, defended the idea of childhood innocence. They attempted to reconcile this idea with the cultural tastes of real children by suggesting that the creators of this type of culture somehow seduced children into liking stories that dealt with such topics as violence, crime, and sexuality. The reformers who expressed this idea went on to argue that children were therefore corrupted by this type of culture. They insisted that this corruptive process accounted for the existence of juvenile delinquency and other not-so-innocent forms of childhood behavior. This line of reasoning first surfaced during the campaign against children's dime novels.

2.

Anthony Comstock's Crusade Against Dime Novels

When the proprietors of the Beadle and Adams publishing firm began marketing dime novels in the early 1860s, they had no idea that they were laying the groundwork for the first major controversy in the history of American children's culture. Indeed, initially they gave little thought to the idea of publishing books for children. They attempted, instead, to appeal to the reading tastes of working-class adults. Some children, however, were attracted to the melodramatic adventure stories that Beadle and Adams published, and because these books were so inexpensive, a number of children began purchasing their own copies. At first Beadle and Adams and the other publishers of dime novels paid little attention to their younger customers, but in the mid-1870s it occurred to them that handsome profits could be made by catering to the juvenile market. Thus, in 1877 Beadle and Adams brought out a new line of stories intended specifically for children. The publications sold for a nickel apiece and were called the *Half-Dime Series*. Other publishers quickly followed suit, and soon newsstands carried a wide assortment of dime novels, half-dime novels, story papers, and boys' papers aimed at children.[1]

Because the publishers of children's dime novels were primarily interested in making money, they tended to publish books that they thought children would buy rather than books that

8

would garner the approval of parents. These publishers urged their writers to imitate those dime novels that had already proven themselves on the juvenile market. Consequently, children's dime novels began to follow discernible formulas. The earliest dime novels intended for children generally dealt with western themes. The plots of these novels revolved around simplistic moral conflicts between virtuous heroes and treacherous Indians or outlaws. Instead of developing their characters' personalities, the authors of these books concentrated on providing numerous exciting and violent action scenes. In the early 1880s, dime-novel publishers began adding detective stories to their juvenile lines. Although these stories were usually set in urban areas, their plots and characters were very similar to those found in dime-novel westerns. Many of the heroes in children's dime novels were not much older than the books' readers, a fact that W.H. Bishop emphasized in an interesting 1879 *Atlantic Monthly* article: "The heroes are boys, and there are few departments of unusual existence in which they are not seen figuring to brilliant advantage."[2]

Dime novels, although popular with thousands of children, were not well-liked by some adults. The most prominent figure among the early critics of dime novels was the famous crusader for moral purity, Anthony Comstock. As founder of the New York Society for the Suppression of Vice and author of the federal anti-obscenity law of 1873, Comstock had enough power and prestige to wage a vigorous campaign against dime novels. He began denouncing this form of children's literature in 1878 and continued his attacks throughout the 1880s. His objections to dime novels received a considerable amount of attention, especially from those who shared his conservative political views and fundamentalist religious beliefs.

Comstock's crusading spirit surfaced well before he began his campaign against dime novels. During his teenage years in New Canaan, Connecticut, he developed a preoccupation with religion. Having regularly attended the community's congregational church throughout his childhood, he was very familiar with the Bible, and he tended to view it as a factual and incontrovertible document. Biblical teachings about sin were of particular interest to Comstock. He often worried about his own sinful inclinations, and he was not entirely certain that his sins would be forgiven. These concerns led him to take an aggressive approach to resisting sin. For example, not long after he allowed himself to be talked into drinking a friend's home-made wine, he broke into the local saloon-keeper's storeroom and spilled all of the kegs of liquor on the floor. Before leaving he wrote a note to the saloon-keeper in which he told the man that unless the saloon was closed the building would be destroyed.

In 1863, at the age of nineteen, Comstock enlisted in the Union army where he continued his battle against drinking. Shocked that whiskey was included among the rations for each soldier, Comstock attempted to convince his companions not to drink it. After this approach failed, he regularly accepted his share of whiskey and then poured it on the ground in front of the other soldiers. Drinking, however, was not the only sin that concerned Comstock during the war years. Lust, masturbation, and the reading of pornography also worried the young soldier. In the diary that he kept during this period he often confessed to a nameless sin, which, in the opinion of his biographers, was probably masturbation.[3] The following entries were typical:

Again tempted and found wanting. Sin, sin. Oh how much peace and happiness is sacrificed on thy altar. Seemed as though Devil had full sway over me today, went right into temptation, and then, Oh such love, Jesus snatched it away out of my reach. How good is he, how sinful am I. I am the chief of sinners, but I should be so miserable and wretched, were it not that God is merciful and I may be forgiven. Glory be to God in the highest.

O I deplore my sinful weak nature so much. If I could but live without sin, I should be the happiest soul living: But Sin, that foe that is ever lurking, stealing happiness from me. What a day will it be when that roaring Lion shall be bound and his wanderings cease, then will we have rest, the glorious rest from sin. O hasten ever welcome day, dawn on our souls.

This morning were severely tempted by Satan and after some time in my own weakness I failed.[4]

Comstock was mustered out of the army in 1865, and a few years later he moved to New York City where he found a job in a dry goods store. During this period he continued his obsession with pornography and other manifestations of sexuality which he considered to be sinful. A number of his acquaintances, he discovered, read erotic literature, and he concluded that this reading material was having a demoralizing effect upon them. He felt so strongly about this issue that in 1868 he began a campaign to rid the city of its pornography dealers and publishers. Initially, he encouraged the police to enforce existing laws against pornography, but he soon decided that this approach was inadequate. Comstock felt that most of the city's police officers showed too little enthusiasm for this area of law enforcement and that the federal and state laws dealing with pornography were too lax. In an effort to correct this situation, he formed an alliance with the leaders of the New York branch of the Young Men's Christian Association (YMCA), and with their backing he traveled to the nation's capital to lobby for a bill that would prohibit producers of obscene materials from using the postal system to distribute their wares. The bill passed, and the postmaster general asked Comstock to supervise its enforcement, a task which Comstock agreed to perform without pay.

Interpreting his victory in Washington, D.C., as a sign that God wanted him to continue his war against pornography, Comstock returned to New York feeling determined to do everything in his power to make American society conform to his conception of moral purity. For its part, society, caught up in the prudery of the Victorian period, was remarkably obliging. In order to carry out his crusade, Comstock felt that he needed the backing of an effective organization. Thus, with the help of a number of his friends from the YMCA, he formed the New York Society for the Suppression of Vice. The organization was incorporated in May 1873, at which time the New York state legislature gave it the legal authority to conduct criminal investigations and make arrests. The incorporators of the society asked Comstock to serve as the organization's secretary and chief special agent and offered him a yearly salary. Since this was a full-time position, Comstock severed his connections with the dry goods business and began dedicating nearly all of his working hours to suppressing vice. During the early years of the organization's existence, Comstock primarily concerned himself with arresting publishers and sellers of pornographic materials, although he also arrested people for performing abortions, selling contraceptives, and running lotteries. He filled the first three annual reports of the society with boasts about how many people he had arrested and how many tons of pornographic books he had confiscated.[5]

Although the suppression of pornography continued to preoccupy Comstock for the rest of his life, his thoughts on censorship, as reflected in the *Fourth Annual Report* of the society, expanded in 1878. He argued that other forms of literature deserved to be condemned along with pornography. Included on his expanded list of objectionable reading materials were children's dime novels. In his first denouncement of dime novels, Comstock grouped atheistic publications, writings by free-love advocates, and dime novels together. All of these types of literature, Comstock maintained, corrupted youth and contributed to anarchy. The specific charges that he made against dime novels, however, were vague and not as severe as the charges that he brought against pornography. Addressing his readers on the subject of dime novels, he wrote, "It should be observed with deepest concern by all friends of virtue, that some of the so-called boys' papers published in this city are pregnant with mischief."[6]

By 1880, Comstock came to the conclusion that dime novels posed a far greater danger than simply encouraging children to behave mischievously. As his hostility toward dime novels increased, Comstock began devoting a considerable amount of space in the society's annual reports to assaults upon this form of children's literature. The arguments against dime novels that Comstock presented in the annual reports generally fell into two categories. One of Comstock's most frequently repeated claims was that dime novels had a "demoralizing influence upon the young mind."[7] These stories, he argued, aroused sexual thoughts and created "an appetite for publications of a grosser type."[8] His other main accusation was that dime novels caused children to commit criminal acts. In the *Sixth Annual Report*, for example, he stated:

> These papers are sold everywhere, and at a price that brings them within reach of any child. They are stories

of criminal life. The leading characters are youthful criminals, who revel in the haunts of iniquity. . . . Read before the intellect is quickened or judgment matured sufficient to show the harm of dwelling on these things, they educate our youth in all the odious features of crime. . . . What is the result? The knife, the dagger and the bludgeon used in the sinks of iniquity, and by hardened criminals, are also found in the schoolroom, the house and the playground of tender youth. Our Court rooms are thronged with infant criminals—with baby felons.[9]

In an attempt to substantiate his charge that dime novels bred juvenile delinquents, Comstock filled several pages of the *Sixth Annual Report* with examples of children who he claimed were led astray by reading dime novels. A boy whom Comstock arrested for selling pornography reportedly pointed to a stack of dime novels found in his room and exclaimed, "There, there's the cause of my ruin—that has cursed me and brought me to this!"[10] Another case that Comstock related involved a young dime-novel reader who stole money from his employer. After being caught, the boy explained that he had "never thought of doing wrong till he read these stories."[11]

When the time came for Comstock to prepare the society's *Ninth Annual Report*, he characterized dime novels as the primary cause of juvenile delinquency. He based this conclusion on a series of interviews that he conducted with a group of young lawbreakers. These children, Comstock reported, "were unanimous in charging their conduct to the cheap stories of crime."[12] Although these children may have been using dime novels as a convenient excuse for their own misbehavior, Comstock accepted their confessions without question and then offered them as evidence that the "vast majority" of crimes committed by juveniles were "the direct result of evil reading."[13]

By choosing the pages of the society's annual reports to denounce dime novels, Comstock was guaranteed a sympathetic audience, for the only people who read these reports were the members of the society and perhaps a few journalists. Comstock decided, however, that his feelings toward dime novels needed to be heard by more than a small group of New Yorkers who were already familiar with his position on children's reading materials. For this reason, he presented his case against dime novels in his second book, *Traps for the Young*, which came out in 1883. As Comstock explained in the preface to the book, *Traps for the Young* was "designed to awaken thought upon the subject of *Evil Reading*, and to expose to the minds of parents, teachers, guardians, and pastors, some of the mighty forces for evil that are today exerting a controlling influence over the young."[14]

In *Traps for the Young*, Comstock repeated much of what he had already said about dime novels in the society's annual reports. Rather than make a series of new charges against dime novels, he simply provided page after page of examples of children who were, according to Comstock, ruined by reading this type of material. Comstock did, however, provide one additional reason for banning dime novels. He argued that the sudden successes that blessed the lives of many dime-novel heroes undermined the willingness of children to work:

> What young man will serve an apprenticeship, working early and late, if his mind is filled with the idea that sudden wealth may be acquired by following the hero of the story? In real life, to begin at the foot of the ladder and work up, step by step, is the rule; but in these stories, inexperienced youth with no moral character, take the foremost positions, and by trick and device, knife and revolver, bribery and corruption, carry everything before them, lifting themselves in a few short weeks to positions of ease and affluence.[15]

Comstock concluded his chapter on dime novels by asking his readers to join in efforts to suppress this form of literature. He urged everyone who disapproved of dime novels to call for the passage of laws that would prohibit or restrict their publication and distribution. Although Comstock felt that passing such laws was the most desirable way to eliminate dime novels, he argued for the implementation of other methods of combating this "evil" as well. He instructed parents to confiscate and burn all dime novels that their children brought home. He also suggested that parents apply economic pressure against businesses that sold dime novels. "The remedy lies in your hands," he told his readers, "by not patronizing any person who offers these death-traps for sale. . . . Let your newsdealer feel that, just in proportion as he prunes his stock of that which is vicious, your interest in his welfare increases and your patronage becomes more constant."[16]

In addition to attacking dime novels in his writings, Comstock frequently voiced his objections to these publications in lecture halls. In 1882 alone, according to the society's *Eighth Annual Report*, Comstock addressed fifteen public meetings during which he warned parents not to allow their children to read dime novels. These lectures were delivered in various locations in New York City as well as in several other cities in the state.[17] On 28 February 1882, a reporter from the *New York Times* attended one of these lectures, and his account of it was published in the next day's paper. According to the reporter, Comstock's lecture lasted for two hours and was attended by a "large audience." Comstock, the reporter noted, "was especially severe upon boys' and girls' weekly story papers which assume to be respectable." The reporter also mentioned that Comstock "related many incidents to show that boys and girls had become criminals through reading the stories in these papers."[18]

Comstock's campaign against dime novels had repercussions outside the state boundaries of New York. Following the successful establishment of the New York Society for the Suppression of Vice, anti-vice societies were founded in Massachusetts, Pennsylvania, Ohio, and several other states. The leaders of these societies paid close attention to Comstock's denouncements of dime novels and often waged their own battles against these publications. In 1885, for example, Boston's Watch and Ward Society convinced the Massachusetts legislature to pass a bill that forbade children from purchasing books and magazines that featured "criminal news, police reports, or accounts of criminal deeds, or pictures and stories of lust or crime."[19]

Joseph W. Leeds, a prominent member of the Philadelphia Purity Alliance and a staunch supporter of Comstock, tried to persuade the Pennsylvania legislature to pass a bill that empowered mayors to outlaw the selling of dime novels in their cities. Although this bill did not become law in Pennsylvania, Leeds and Comstock lobbied for the passage of similar bills in state legislatures across the country. Their efforts met with success in California, Connecticut, Maine, New Hampshire, South Carolina, Tennessee, and Washington.[20] Leeds also expanded upon Comstock's list of alternatives to dime novels. Whereas Comstock simply recommended that children read the Bible, history, or "some wholesome tale,"[21] Leeds compiled a list of "acceptable" children's periodicals and distributed it to the editors of 275 newspapers.[22] Thus, although Comstock and his supporters did not succeed in forcing the publishers of dime novels out of business, they did manage to make the reading of dime novels by children an issue of public concern.

Any attempt to explain why Comstock thought that dime novels were nearly as objectionable as pornography must take into account his views on human sexuality. From his adolescence onward, sexuality was a source of anxiety for Comstock. He found it impossible to accept sexuality as a natural part of life, but he found it equally impossible to ignore it. Comstock's anxieties about sexuality led him to view it as a serious threat to his own self-concept as well as to the entirety of civilization. In describing this threat, he proclaimed that "there is no force at work in the community more insidious, more constant in its demands, or more powerful and far-reaching than lust."[23] Comstock apparently believed that sexuality was the root cause of all criminal and antisocial behavior, for in *Traps for the Young* he repeatedly stated that "lust is the boon companion of all other crimes."[24] Because of this belief, Comstock felt that the suppression of libidinal drives was the key to reducing all forms of crime and undesirable conduct. Consequently, he advised adults that unless they were primarily interested in procreation, they should abstain from all sexually related activities.

Comstock attempted to follow his own advice. There is no indication that he engaged in any sexual activities other than masturbation until his late twenties, and his Civil War diaries suggest that he felt immense guilt whenever he did masturbate. When he finally married, it was to a woman who was more of a mother figure than a lover. At the time of their marriage, she was ten years his senior and in poor health. Within their first year of marriage they had a daughter. But the child died while still in infancy, and they apparently made no effort to have any more children. As much as Comstock wanted to renounce his own sexuality, however, he was unable to banish sexual thoughts from his mind. In an attempt to deal with this part of himself which he hated, he projected it upon the devil.[25] Satan, he told himself and his readers, was responsible for the arousal of nearly all sexual feelings.

For Comstock, the devil was not a vague abstraction. He felt that he knew the devil well. He constantly referred to Satan in both his private and public writings, and he often claimed to have special insights into the devil's desires and methods. Comstock was aware, though, that not everyone believed in the existence of the devil, and in the final pages of *Traps for the Young* he attempted to accommodate those people who did not share his beliefs about Satan:

> It may not be pleasant or popular to speak of a devil, or of his having a kingdom and power; but I doubt if any man could go through the experiences of my past eleven years and not be thoroughly persuaded that there is one, and that he has numerous agencies actively employed recruiting for his kingdom. . . .
>
> I believe that there is a devil. Those who disagree with me in this may translate my language. All I ask is that they admit the vital truth on which I insist. Let my language be considered symbolical, provided the evils I denounce are regarded as *diabolical*.[26]

Because Comstock associated sexuality with the devil, he tended to think of sexual interests as being unnatural. The fact that most people had such interests only proved, Comstock argued, that the devil possessed tremendous power as a corrupter of souls.

Comstock's acceptance of this line of reasoning led him to argue that human beings begin life uncorrupted. Thus, Comstock felt compelled to champion the myth of childhood innocence. On several occasions he argued that sexuality was not a normal attribute of childhood. God, in Comstock's opinion, did not intend for children to be interested in sex. Indeed, Comstock maintained that when God created children, He meant for them to be innocent of all sinful impulses. Comstock underscored this point by comparing children to a glass of sparkling water:

> Fill a clean, clear glass with water and hold it to the light, and you cannot perceive a single discoloration. It will sparkle like a gem, seeming to rejoice in its purity,

and dance in the sunlight, because of its freedom from pollution. So with a child. Its innocence bubbles all over with glee. What is more sweet, fascinating, and beautiful than a pure, innocent child?[27]

The greatest challenge facing parents and other adults who cared for children, according to Comstock, was to preserve childhood innocence. This task, he explained, required constant attention because children's mental powers, unlike those of Christian adults, were not strong enough to detect the subtle traps that the devil placed before them. Another factor that made this task even more difficult was that Comstock's devil specialized in corrupting children. In *Traps for the Young*, Comstock provided the following explanation for Satan's special interest in children:

The world is the devil's hunting-ground, and children are his choicest game. All along their pathway the merciless hunter sets his traps, and they are set with a certainty of a large return. To corrupt a boy or girl, he knows lessens the chance for a pure man or woman. If at the beginning of life the mind and soul be defiled, he reckons that the youth will become in the community a sure agent to drag others down.[28]

Throughout his career, Comstock maintained that Satan's favorite method of corrupting children was to expose them to pernicious reading materials. Comstock's devil realized, however, that because his pet trap, pornography, was "so libidinous," most adults would not allow children to buy or read it.[29] In order to avoid this obstacle, Satan, according to Comstock, had his agents create "a series of new snares of fascinating construction, small and tempting in price, and baited with high-sounding names." These new traps, Comstock went on to explain, comprised "a large variety of half-dime novels, five and ten cent story papers, and low-priced pamphlets for boys and girls."[30] It was Comstock's contention that Satan attempted to lull parents into believing that dime novels were harmless by not including specific references to sexuality in their pages. Claiming to see through this ploy, Comstock argued that dime novels were filled with accounts of crimes because Satan knew that all crimes involved lust. For this reason, Comstock was certain that after children developed a taste for stories about criminals, they would quickly succumb to other devil-traps, including pornography. Thus, even though dime novels hardly ever mentioned sexuality, they were, in Comstock's mind, little better than pornographic works and therefore deserved his condemnation. In other words, he viewed his campaign against dime novels as a natural extension of his purity crusade. Since this crusade was clearly fueled by his anxieties about sexuality, there can be little doubt that his stand on dime novels was tied to his life-long struggle to control his own libidinal drives. It is also likely that his anxieties were shared by many of the people who so enthusiastically supported his various crusades.

3.

The Response of Children's Librarians to Dime Novels and Series Books

The years during which Comstock waged his purity crusade also witnessed an intensification of efforts to "professionalize" medicine, law, business, education, and various other sectors of American society. This development had a profound impact on the history of American childhood. Child-rearing, which had previously been thought of as being essentially a family matter, attracted the attention of numerous "professionals." Social workers became interested in children's home and work environments. Public health officials expressed concern over children's consumption of contaminated milk and water, while pediatricians advocated reforms in infant hygiene and nutrition. G. Stanley Hall and other psychologists argued that the child-rearing process should reflect the latest theories on the psychological development of children. Nearly all of these "professionals" felt that because of their special training, they were better qualified than many parents to make certain child-rearing decisions.[1]

Librarians were among the "professionals" who became interested in child rearing during the late nineteenth century. In the 1870s and '80s, public libraries began opening their doors to children. Numerous libraries from this period added children's books to their collections, and some even set aside a corner or a small room for children to use. Although most libraries did not hire special librarians to work with children until the 1890s or early 1900s, children's literature began attracting the attention of general librarians as early as the mid-1870s. An increasing number of librarians believed that children's reading materials shaped their young readers' minds, and because of this belief, some felt that it was their duty to make certain that children read nothing but "wholesome" literature. In an effort to achieve this goal, some librarians wrote books of literary criticism on children's literature and promoted the introduction of courses on children's literature on college campuses.[2] On another level, though, the idea that children should read only "quality" books caused a number of librarians to suppress children's books that they judged to be unwholesome. The leaders of this campaign frequently expressed their views on children's literature in articles published in the *Library Journal* and in other periodicals intended for librarians. In the process of writing these articles, librarians from the turn of the century contributed to the growing body of prescriptive literature on child-rearing written by America's "professional" elite.

Several librarians from the 1870s and '80s shared Comstock's concerns about dime novels. Like Comstock, these librarians argued that the exciting plots, violent action scenes, depraved villains, and omnipotent heroes found in many dime novels had a corruptive influence on the minds of juvenile readers. The charges that librarians made against dime novels ranged from ruining children's reading tastes to causing children to engage in criminal behavior. The editors of the *Library Journal* reprinted a number of newspaper articles in which the reading of dime novels was cited as the reason that children engaged in wrongdoing. In one such article, it was reported that a fourteen-year-old boy "shot himself during a period of mental aberration caused by reading dime novels."[3] Another article noted that dime novels caused three boys to run away to "Texas to be wild rovers on the plains."[4]

Librarians from this period employed a variety of tactics in their attempts to suppress dime novels, the most common of which was simply to ban dime novels from library shelves. Other children's books that, in the opinion of librarians, resembled dime novels were also banned. Two books that were often placed in this category were Mark Twain's *The Adventures of Tom*

Sawyer and *The Adventures of Huckleberry Finn*. Several librarians objected to these books because Twain portrayed some of his adult characters in a negative light and allowed his boy heroes to misbehave with impunity. Many librarians refused to purchase Twain's books, and others removed his books after reading them.[5] The librarians at the public library in Concord, Massachusetts, for example, decided to take *The Adventures of Huckleberry Finn* out of circulation, a move that received praise from the editor of the *Springfield Republican*. In an editorial reprinted in the *New York Times*, the editor noted:

> The Concord public library committee deserve well of the public by their action in banishing Mark Twain's new book, *Huckleberry Finn*, on the ground that it's trashy and vicious. It is time that this influential pseudonym should cease to carry into homes and libraries unworthy productions. . . . [*Tom Sawyer* and *Huckleberry Finn*] are no better in tone than the dime novels which flood the blood-and-thunder reading population. Mr. Clemens has made them smarter, for he has an inexhaustible fund of "quips and cranks and wanton wiles," and his literary skill is, of course, superior, but their moral level is low, and their perusal cannot be anything less than harmful.[6]

Some librarians devised unique methods of discouraging children from reading dime novels. Minerva L. Saunders, who worked for the public library in Pawtucket, Rhode Island, was one such librarian. According to an article that Saunders wrote for the *Library Journal*, she noticed that a number of children who used the library's reading room did not peruse books owned by the library. Instead, they read dime novels which they concealed in between the covers of bona fide library books. Whenever Saunders spotted children reading dime novels, she made it a point to tell "them the dangers of reading the stuff." Her lectures, however, "seemed to have little effect." In an effort to devise a more effective method of persuading children not to read dime novels, Saunders, together with W. R. Sayles, a trustee of the library, decided to employ scare tactics. Saunders and Sayles purchased a scrapbook which they filled with "clippings from newspapers at home and abroad, concerning the pernicious effect upon boys of reading such literature and especially items of police news . . . in which the dime novel was the inspiration to the unlawful deeds which brought the little fellows into the clutches of the police, or into danger and trouble." After completing the scrapbook, Saunders would require every child she caught with a dime novel to read the clippings in it. She reported that after reading these articles the offending child "was willing to give up his dime novel and be guided in the selection of his reading material."[7]

During the 1870s and '80s, most librarians who published articles on children's literature felt that librarians should guide children toward respected works of literature and nonfiction. They divided children's reading materials into gradations of desirability. Dime novels were generally classified as being the least desirable, while biographies, scientific publications, history books, and classic works of literature were thought of as being the most desirable. Although nearly all librarians felt that children should always be encouraged to upgrade the quality of their book selections, a number of librarians believed that children could not be immediately transformed from dime-novel readers into lovers of Shakespeare. The most effective method of curing inveterate consumers of dime novels, in the opinion of these librarians, was to entice them to read books that were similar to dime novels but less violent and vulgar. Only after accomplishing this goal, according to this line of reasoning, could librarians succeed in convincing children to check out books by reputable authors.

Samuel S. Green, a librarian from Worcester, Massachusetts, presented the case for providing children with some "exciting" books in an article entitled "Sensational Fiction in Public Libraries," which appeared in the *Library Journal* in September 1879:

> In order to keep boys and girls from reading . . . [dime novels], we must give them interesting books that are better. But sensational books in the circulating departments of our public libraries do good in another way. They give young persons a taste for reading. . . . If boys and girls grow up with a dislike of reading, or without feeling attracted towards this occupation, they will not read anything. But if a love of reading has been cultivated by giving them when young such books as they

will enjoy reading, then they will turn naturally to reading as an employment of their leisure, and will read such
books as correspond to the grade of culture and the
stage of intellectual development reached by them. They
will thus be saved from idleness and vice.[8]

Heading Green's list of recommended "sensational" stories
were the scores of popular children's books written by Horatio
Alger and Oliver Optic, whose real name was William Taylor
Adams. Alger's rags-to-riches tales and Optic's adventure stories
generally featured fast paced plots and unusually competent child
heroes, but unlike dime novels, they also included moralistic
elements. Although Green felt that Alger's and Optic's books had
"little literary merit," he argued that they were "written by men
who mean well."[9] Green believed that as long as children eventually moved beyond Alger's and Optic's books, librarians did
not need to worry about allowing children to read them.

In addition to Green, several other librarians defended Alger
and Optic as stepping-stones on the road to more respectable
literature. Minerva L. Saunders of Pawtucket, for example, wrote
that she found "that after boys have had either a small or a full
dose of Alger, they are very ready to be promoted to something
more substantial."[10] A librarian from the Boston Public Library
expressed a similar view when asked about working with children:

Give them interesting books (Optic and Alger, if needs
be), and you fix their attention. Above all, let the book
be interesting; for the attention is never fixed by, nor
does the memory ever retain, what is laborious to read.
But, once assured of their devotion, with their confidence secured and their attention fixed, there is nothing
to prevent the work of direction succeeding admirably
with them.[11]

The fact that Alger's and Optic's books were widely circulated in
public libraries during the 1870s and '80s could suggest that a
large number of librarians held similar opinions of these books.[12]

In the 1890s, however, Alger and Optic fell into disrepute
among a growing number of librarians. This development was
tied to the emergence of a group of librarians who specialized in

working with children, several of whom played prominent roles in the American Library Association.[13] Unlike Green and the other librarians who defended Alger and Optic, these children's librarians felt that children should be sheltered from unrealistic descriptions of daily life as well as from stories of violence and crime. This position was first articulated by Martha H. Brooks, a member of the Ladies' Commission on Sunday School Books, in 1879. In an article entitled "Sunday School Libraries," she argued that if a child desired adventure stories, librarians should give him or her "bright, crisp narratives of real life and adventure." In her opinion, once such a child has read books about "what men and boys have done already in Arctic Sea or Great Desert, on mountain heights or in depths of forests, he will not need to seek for fictitious adventure."[14] As the 1880s progressed, Brooks's stand on "sensational" fiction gradually gained a following, and by the mid-1890s nearly every children's librarian who published an article on this issue agreed with her position.

Rather than use Alger's and Optic's books to encourage children to read, children's librarians from the turn of the century attempted to entice children to read historical fiction, travel stories, and various other forms of nonfiction. Biographies were viewed as being ideal reading material for children by a considerable number of librarians, some of whom went to great lengths to persuade children to check out biographical works. For example, Clara W. Hunt, a children's librarian from Newark, New Jersey, removed the word "biography" from the top of her list of recommended biographies and replaced it with the following heading: "Would you like to read about heroes of the olden time, brave engineers and sailors, beautiful princesses and girls who could sing like the birds? Here is a list of such books."[15]

Although children's librarians from this period frequently argued that children's literature should be true to life, they were not opposed to all forms of fantasy. Overt fantasies, such as Lewis Carroll's *Alice's Adventures in Wonderland*, rarely received criticism from librarians, and the fantastic elements in classic fairy tales were generally thought to be harmless, although some librarians disliked the violence found in many of them.[16] On the whole, children's librarians tended to approve of fanciful children's literature in which the fantasy elements were confined to an imaginary world or a distant time in the past, but they strongly disapproved of children's books in which fantasy elements were interjected into realistic settings. Librarians especially objected to books that featured unrealistically drawn heroes, such as those found in Alger's and Optic's books. Even though Alger and Optic imbued their stories with moral lessons, they both created young heroes who often dealt with adults as equals. In an article published in 1907, Grace Thompson of the Brooklyn Public Library explained why she and her colleagues frowned upon the adult-like heroes whom Alger and other authors created:

> There are still people who uphold the Alger books as creating a reading habit. In genuine experience they create only an Alger reading habit. But worse than this is their effect to rob childhood of its joyousness. . . . Their boys and girls are really business men and women. . . . Boys and girls, particularly boys and girls in our cities, do often have to be business men and women. Let them learn wisdom in these lines from experience. When they come to the library let them find that life is not all business, some of it is pure enjoyment. What child needs to read of happy childhood or of fairyland more than the elder brothers and little mothers.[17]

Thompson's comments reflected an attitude toward children that was held by a number of other children's librarians. According to these librarians' conception of child psychology, childhood was not only a time of innocence but was also a time of "joyousness." They felt that children should be content with their lot and not wish to enter the adult world prematurely. Because of this attitude, children's librarians from the early 1900s tended to look askance at all children's books that contained child heroes who transcended the restrictions facing normal children. Thus, even though children often sought out such books and gave every appearance of enjoying them, Thompson and those who agreed with her felt compelled to argue that the pleasure which young readers derived from these books was of an "inferior" nature. The only books that were capable of providing children with "pure enjoyment," in their opinion, were those that supported their notion of childhood happiness and contentment.

Despite the charges that Thompson and others brought

against books by Alger and Optic, dime novels remained the chief target of children's librarians from the 1890s and early 1900s. This situation began to change, however, around 1910. In response to the controversy surrounding dime novels, the United States Postal Service revoked the second-class mailing permits of many dime novel publishers. This move, combined with the emergence of pulp magazines, convinced most publishers to stop producing and marketing dime novels.[18] The pulp magazines that took the place of dime novels on American newsstands were just as violent as their predecessors, but because they were aimed primarily at adult readers, children's librarians tended to ignore them.

At the same time that dime novels were disappearing, the sales of children's books modeled after Alger's and Optic's novels escalated. These publications were generally referred to as "series books" because the same characters reappeared in volume after volume. Although series books cost more than dime novels, they were still within the financial reach of many youngsters, and they were frequently sold directly to children. The publishers of these books attempted to attract a diverse audience by offering consumers a variety of heroes, ranging from the gunslinging cowboys found in the *Pony Rider Boys Series* to the reasonably well-behaved students found in the *Grammar School Boys Series*. Numerous publishers also marketed serials intended for girl readers, including the *Girl Aviators Series*, the *Bobbsey Twins* books, and the *Automobile Girls Series*.[19]

As the popularity of dime novels waned, children's librarians began to view series books as the form of children's literature that most deserved their condemnation. In article after article, children's librarians from the 1910s and '20s accused series books of being "trivial"[20] and "hopelessly mediocre."[21] According to these librarians, series books not only stunted children's "capacity for mental effort in reading,"[22] but they also gave children "a false ideal of life."[23] Some librarians made other charges against series books. For instance, Caroline Burnite, the Director of Children's Work at the Cleveland Public Library, maintained that these books fostered "social prejudice" and encouraged a "belief in fate."[24] Burnite especially disliked girls' series books that dealt with love themes:

For girls, such books contain views of social life, and the relations of individuals toward one another which are almost entirely false. The love interest is always the theme, envy is usually the mainspring; the scene usually shifts from one of poverty to extreme wealth. They foster in an inexperienced young girl a dangerous trust in strangers and blunt any inherent acumen on the part of the reader as to any possible channels for her own life to work out. Largely, I think, because this class of literature is so entirely a repetition of theme and situation, the thread connecting it with good literature is almost impossible to find.[25]

Mary E. S. Root, a prominent figure among American librarians, brought the movement to eliminate series books from public libraries to a head in 1929. On behalf of her fellow children's librarians, Root compiled a list of "books in series not circulated by standardized libraries,"[26] which the editors of the *Wilson Bulletin*, a professional journal for librarians, published in January 1929. Included on Root's list were the works of over sixty authors. Popular boys' series, such as Victor Appleton's *Tom Swift* books, Robert Drake's *Boy Allies* stories, and Herbert Carter's *Boy Scout Series* received Root's censure. Girls' series books fared no better. Among the serial books for girls that Root condemned were Laura Lee Hope's *Bobbsey Twins* books, Gertrude W. Morrison's *Girls of Central High Series*, and Nell Speed's *Molly Brown* stories. Root also recommended that libraries ban a number of children's books by nineteenth-century authors, including those by Horatio Alger, Oliver Optic, Harry Castlemon, and Martha Finley.

Although Root's list was intended for the eyes of librarians, Ernest F. Ayres, the owner of a bookstore in Boise, Idaho, happened to come across it. His negative reaction to Root's list led him to write an article for the *Wilson Bulletin* in which he defended children's series books. He stated that he read some of these books as a child, and he felt that they had no harmful effect upon him. He then went on to ask, "Is it the place of any librarian, holding a position as trustee of public funds, to tell men and women who enjoyed those books when they were young, that their children shall not be allowed to read the same tales?"[27]

After the publication of Ayres's article, the editorial office of the *Wilson Bulletin* received several responses from children's librarians who felt compelled to address the question that Ayres raised. These responses brought into focus the elitist attitude that many children's librarians had toward parents. Lillian Herron Mitchell, for example, argued that the only parents who would consider providing series books for their children were those who were "below average in education."[28] She dismissed Ayres's argument that children should be allowed to read the same books that their parents enjoyed by simply stating that "the really intelligent man or woman who was raised on this series stuff doesn't want sonny to waste any time on it."[29] Mitchell reasoned that children's librarians had to select reading material for children of uneducated parents because, in her opinion, these parents were incapable of evaluating children's literature. "After all," she wrote, "librarians know that the best test of a good child's book is whether a literary minded adult will enjoy it or not. By literary minded, I mean one who appreciates the worthwhile in literature."[30] Since Mitchell was confident that uneducated parents did not meet the criteria she set for being literary minded, she had no qualms about disregarding their opinions on children's literature.

In addition to sparking a lively debate in the pages of the *Wilson Bulletin*, the publication of Root's list of condemned books marked the culmination of a half-century campaign on the part of several children's librarians to suppress dime novels and series books, in the process of which, these librarians made a statement about their attitudes toward children. They believed, along with Comstock, that children's surroundings largely determined the nature of children's thought patterns and behavior. Consequently, they assumed that references to violence and crime in children's literature introduced young readers to the concept of violence and increased the likelihood that children would engage in violent or criminal acts. By working to eliminate dime novels and other forms of children's literature that contained violent themes, librarians felt that they were protecting innocent minds and helping to reduce juvenile delinquency.

Children's librarians' objections to series books, however, were based on beliefs that were somewhat different from those espoused by Comstock. While Comstock might have agreed with the librarians' charge that the unrealistically drawn child heroes found in series books were too adult-like, it is doubtful that he would have felt that reading about such characters would arouse feelings of discontent that would spoil children's happiness. Comstock seldom wrote about happiness, and he usually did not equate it with innocence. Indeed, for Comstock, innocence was typified more by solemnness than mirth. Children's librarians, though, tended to think of childhood as the most joyful time in life, and they felt that children's literature should support this conception of childhood. In articulating this belief, they associated happiness and contentment with the myth of childhood innocence.

The differences between Comstock's beliefs about childhood and the beliefs held by children's librarians paralleled the differences between Locke's and Rousseau's conceptions of childhood innocence. Both Locke and Comstock felt that children's minds were blank at birth, but neither believed that children were endowed with inborn positive traits. In the opinions of these two men, children's personalities were totally malleable. They felt that children could be made into demons as well as angels. Children's librarians, however, tended to agree with the Rousseauean notion that childhood innocence was more than a state of "blankness". Like Rousseau, these librarians felt that children were naturally good until they were corrupted by society, and that uncorrupted children were uniformly content and happy.

The fact that these librarians clung to a view of childhood as a period of blissfulness when they were constantly presented with evidence that many children sought out books that contradicted this view requires an explanation. One possible reason is that these librarians wanted to believe that their own childhoods were innocent and happy and therefore became defensive when their beliefs about childhood were challenged. Also, since the majority of these librarians never had children of their own, they may not have had close enough contact with children to be fully aware of the less innocent aspects of children's personalities. Interestingly, Rousseau also was never involved with raising children. This similarity between Rousseau's life and the lives of these librarians suggests that there may be a relationship between childlessness and the tendency to romanticize childhood.

4.

Adult Reactions
to Children's Radio Programs

Shortly after the publication of Mary E. S. Root's list of condemned series books in 1929, children's radio programs emerged. This development was the result of a major innovation in the economic substructure of American children's culture. A few advertisers from the early 1930s brought about this change when they decided to redefine children's role in the marketplace. Rather than view children as passive consumers of products that their parents bought, these advertisers theorized that children were capable of influencing their parents' purchasing decisions and could therefore be thought of as indirect consumers. Some proponents of this perspective attempted to devise ways to create a demand for certain products among children. One method that they considered was radio advertising. Since this approach had been established as a successful way to reach adult consumers, it seemed probable that it would work with children. The best way to reach large numbers of young radio listeners, these advertisers determined, was to sponsor programs intended specifically for children. Thus, in the process of designing advertising campaigns around children, advertisers began to view children's culture as a vehicle through which commercial messages could be conveyed to children.

"Adventure Time with Little Orphan Annie," the first sponsored radio program created for children, made its debut in December of 1930. The sponsor, Ovaltine, discovered that the program helped improve sales of the company's powdered milk supplement and decided to continue sponsoring the show. In 1931, the Kellogg Company began sponsoring a radio version of John Dille's comic strip, "Buck Rogers in the Twenty-Fifth Century," and a few years later General Mills inaugurated a children's program entitled "Jack Armstrong, the All-American Boy." These shows and others soon to join them on the airwaves were designed to attract as many young listeners as possible. For this reason, the producers of these shows, like the authors of dime novels and series books, catered to the children's tastes. Predictably, children's radio programs shared many similarities with these earlier forms of children's culture. The heroes of children's programs generally possessed unnatural strength and courage and were often quite young. The shows' plots revolved around violent conflicts between the heroes and their ruthless enemies, and the action frequently took place in unusual settings. The sounds of fistfights, gunshots, explosions, sirens, and dying people were regularly featured. Each show usually concluded with a suspenseful and indefinite ending designed to draw children back the next day. Although many of these programs succeeded in garnering loyal audiences, they were not well regarded by certain articulate adults. Just as dime novels and series books attracted criticism in their time, children's radio programs became the focus of a heated controversy.[1]

Even though some of the criticisms that were leveled at children's radio programs were similar to charges that had been brought against dime novels and series books, the nature of this controversy differed in some ways from the earlier ones. The campaign against children's radio programs lacked a powerful leader, such as Comstock, and it was not dominated by members of a particular "profession," such as children's librarians. While a number of educators and other "professionals" involved themselves in this campaign, most of the participants were affiliated with either parent groups or women's organizations. Nearly all of them came from middle-class or upper-middle-class backgrounds, but they did not constitute an easily defined group. They did share, however, an interest in child psychology, and they usually attempted to base their arguments on psychological rather than moral grounds. For the most part, their backgrounds in child psychology came not from specific training in the subject, but from the numerous child-rearing manuals and magazines for parents that helped popularize child psychology during the 1930s, '40s, and '50s.[2]

Organized opposition to commercially sponsored children's radio programs first surfaced in Scarsdale, a suburb of New York City. During a Fox Meadow Parent-Teachers Association meeting held in January 1933, a group of mothers from Scarsdale argued that their children were suffering from emotional problems because of these programs. Some mothers claimed that their children had nightmares after hearing these shows; a few reported that their children screamed and wept while listening to the programs. The members of the association decided that these charges deserved serious attention and appointed a committee to "head the movement for saner radio programs for children."[3] This committee, under the leadership of Alma M. Ernst, a housewife and community activist, conducted a survey of children's radio programs and came to the conclusion that nearly half of these programs were "poor" or "very poor." Several of the programs most popular among children received the committee's lowest rating.

Ernst's committee summarized its findings in a published report which was distributed throughout the community and reached the education department of Columbia University. Believing that Ernst's committee raised some important issues, the department's faculty members invited Ernst to deliver a lecture on children's radio programs at the university. Ernst accepted, and arrangements were made for her to speak on 28 February 1933. The *New York Times* covered Ernst's address and published two lengthy articles about the "Scarsdale mothers" and their "campaign against horror stories on the radio."[4] These articles aroused the interest of newspaper and magazine editors from around the nation. Dozens of newspapers covered the story, and several magazines, including the *Nation*, the *Literary Digest*, and *Parents' Magazine*, published editorials supporting the Scarsdale parents.[5]

Clara Savage Littledale, the editor of *Parents' Magazine*, urged her readers to take action against violent and exciting radio

programs for children. In an editorial published in May 1933, she
wrote:

> We are heartily in sympathy with parents who want the
> best for their children. We admire mothers and fathers
> who refuse to grow careless or discouraged or to sit
> back supinely with a "There's-nothing-we-can-do-
> about-it" air. There *is* something that intelligent mothers
> and fathers can do. They can make themselves heard.
> . . . Our advice to parents is: if you are critical of the
> type of program which the radio is supplying for chil-
> dren, *say so*. Write to the sponsors of the program and
> tell them why you object to it.[6]

Hundreds of parents followed Littledale's advice. Not only
did they write letters of protest to the sponsors of children's
programs; they sent letters to the networks, the Federal Communications Commission, and their local newspapers. The *New York
Times*, for example, received a letter from a father who claimed
that radio programs had introduced fear into his six-year-old
son's life. These programs, according to this correspondent,
caused his son to imagine "footsteps in the dark, kidnappers
lurking in every corner and ghosts appearing and disappearing
everywhere and emitting their blood-curdling noises, all in true
radio fashion."[7] In another letter published by the *New York
Times*, Ludmila Jaffee argued that children who listened to radio
programs suffered from "unhealthy excitement, unnecessary
nervousness, irritability, and restless sleep."[8]

In addition to fueling a letter-writing campaign, parental
disapproval of radio programs led to the formation of the Wom-
en's National Radio Committee in 1934.[9] The committee consisted of representatives from twenty-eight women's organizations with a combined membership, according to the *New York
Times*, of 25,000,000.[10] These representatives elected Mrs. Harold V. Milligan as their chair, and she presided over their regularly
scheduled meetings and served as the committee's spokesperson.
In an attempt to encourage broadcasters to refrain from airing
violent children's programs, the committee began publishing a
list of children's programs that won its approval. To be included
on this list, programs had to contain "genuine informational
material" and offer "stimulating mental exercise." Specifically

excluded from this list were programs that were "too exciting" or "too suspenseful." The committee also excluded programs that portrayed children in "abnormal situations."[11]

The Child Study Association of America, a group of educators and psychologists, also became involved in the controversy surrounding children's radio programs. This organization, which was founded by G. Stanley Hall and several other psychologists during the 1893 World's Columbian Exposition in Chicago, contributed to the popularization of child psychology through its many programs and publications.[12] In November 1934, the association organized a symposium concerning radio programs for children. Representatives from numerous child-care agencies attended the symposium and spent many hours discussing the merits of children's programs. Sidonie M. Gruenberg, the director of the association, summarized the feelings of some of the participants at the conclusion of the symposium. "It is beyond dispute that many of the programs are objectionable," she stated, "because they convey false or misleading sentimentalities, or because they murder the King's English or play too recklessly with elemental fears and horrors."[13]

Given the fact that many children's radio programs were nearly as violent as dime novels, it is significant to note that neither Gruenberg nor the other early critics of children's radio programs claimed that these shows caused children to become juvenile delinquents. They deviated from Comstock's line of reasoning by arguing that violent and exciting radio programs increased children's anxieties and fears. The critics of children's radio programs broke away from the idea that violent children's culture corrupted children and embraced instead a notion that this type of culture threatened children's emotional stability. This shift reflected the popularization of child psychology and its impact on middle-class adults' attitudes toward children.

Although sponsors tended to ignore criticisms of their children's programs, the networks felt obliged to respond. The networks feared that if they did not respond they might face pressure from the Federal Communications Commission. Shortly after the parents from Scarsdale began their campaign, executives from the Columbia Broadcasting System (CBS) offered these parents an opportunity to produce their own children's program. Ernst and several members of the Scarsdale Women's Club accepted the offer. With the help of a local school teacher, the group wrote a script about an event that occurred during the American Revolution. Scarsdale's Wayside Players, an amateur theater group, agreed to read the dialogue, and CBS's staff provided technical assistance.[14] The show aired on 19 February 1935 and was greeted with poor reviews. Critics felt that the program was hopelessly amateurish, and a number of children referred to it as being too babyish.[15] In fact, several members of the Scarsdale Women's Club were dissatisfied with the program, and a few even thought it was "terrible."[16] Following the failure of their program, the Scarsdale parents and their campaign against children's radio programs ceased to garner national attention.

Despite the demise of the Scarsdale group, CBS's children's programs continued to draw fire from various parents and child-care "professionals." In response to this controversy, William S. Paley, the president of CBS, decided that the network's programs for children had to meet certain standards. These new standards were outlined in a policy statement that Paley released on 13 May 1935:

> The exalting, as modern heroes, of gangsters, criminals, and racketeers will not be allowed.
>
> Disrespect for either parental or other proper authority must not be glorified or encouraged.
>
> Cruelty, greed, and selfishness must not be presented as worthy motivations.
>
> Programs that arouse harmful nervous reactions in the child must not be presented.
>
> Conceit, smugness, or an unwarranted sense of superiority over others less fortunate may not be presented as laudable.
>
> Recklessness and abandon must not be falsely identified with a healthy spirit of adventure.
>
> Unfair exploitation of others for personal gain must not be made praiseworthy.
>
> Dishonesty and deceit are not to be made appealing or attractive to the child.[17]

CBS's new policy won praise from several quarters. Anning S. Prall, the chairperson of the Federal Communications Commission, referred to it as "an example of wise leadership,"[18] and the Women's National Radio Committee called the move "the beginning of a new era in broadcasting."[19] The leaders of the movement to reform children's radio programs hoped that the National Broadcasting Company (NBC) would soon follow CBS's example. Their hopes, however, were short-lived. In an effort to explain why NBC refused to revamp its children's programs, the network's president, Merlin H. Aylesworth, argued that advertisers were only interested in sponsoring children's programs that attracted large audiences. "Unfortunately," he went on to state, "children are not always interested in the programs in which their parents think they should be interested."[20] Although Aylesworth was on target, most critics of children's radio programs were not satisfied with his response.

To the disappointment of Paley, Aylesworth, and other network executives, the controversy surrounding children's radio programs intensified during the second half of the 1930s. Convinced that NBC and the Mutual Broadcasting System (MBS) were not willing to reform their children's programs, proponents of "wholesome" programming decided to take their complaints to the Federal Communications Commission (FCC). Between 1936 and 1938 the members of the commission received thousands of letters from parents, educators, and physicians demanding that the commission force the networks to stop broadcasting violent and exciting children's programs. Responding to this pressure, Commissioner George Henry Payne publicly condoned the movement to "clean up" children's programs. In a statement released in October 1937, Payne declared that "the radio stations ought to be prevented from pumping into 30,000,000 homes children's programs of such character as they broadcast now."[21]

In 1938, the FCC began pressuring broadcasters to suspend their controversial children's programs. Payne, for example, delivered a speech before the National Conference of Education in which he suggested that broadcasters who aired "harmful" children's programs ought to be denied access to the airwaves.[22] Payne and his fellow commissioners were especially critical of NBC's programming. In November 1938, John F. Royal, NBC's vice-president in charge of programs, was summoned to testify before the commission. He was asked, among other things, to respond to complaints that the network's programs for children were too "sensational" and "nerve-racking." Royal answered by quipping that radio programs were "not to be blamed for all excitable children." His response did not amuse his interrogators.[23]

The Federal Communications Commissioners were not the only reformers who became interested in children's radio programs during the late 1930s. These years also saw an increased involvement on the part of "professionals" in the campaign for "better" children's programming. College professors, pediatricians, and authorities on juvenile delinquency were among the "professionals" who spoke out on this issue. Most of them tended to focus their arguments on the relationship between radio listening and children's psychological development. Relying almost entirely on anecdotal evidence, they concluded that listening to radio programs caused children to suffer from psychological problems. They did not always agree, however, on the specific nature of these problems.

Certain academicians argued that radio listening dulled children's mental processes. Speaking before an audience of educators, Jay B. Nash, a physical education professor at New York University, denounced the networks' children's hour as a waste of leisure time. Nash told his listeners, "It's the moronishness, the stupidity, the inactivity of it, rather than the badness, that gives us the greatest concern."[24] John J. DeBoer of Chicago Teachers College agreed with Nash's assessment of children's programs. DeBoer maintained that children who spent many hours listening to radio programs were less analytical than children who seldom listened to radio shows.[25] He also suggested that radio listening suppressed children's imaginations. "When drama is transferred to the radio," DeBoer wrote, "practically nothing is left to the imagination. . . . Radio supplies the real cries of children, the laughter of men, the ratatat of the machine gun."[26]

Mary I. Preston, a pediatrician from San Francisco, also spoke out against children's programs. In an article published in the *Journal of Pediatrics*, Preston asserted that thousands of children were literally addicted to radio crime programs. The effects of this "addiction" included nervousness, nightmares, eating disturbances, and fingernail biting. Preston admitted, though, that some children who frequently listened to radio programs suffered from none of these problems. She accounted for this phenomenon by suggesting that these children had become cold-hearted and callous:

> It was found that hundreds and hundreds of exposures to the sufferings of others for the purpose of entertainment most fortunately have brought about, in many, many children, an atrophy of such desirable emotions as sympathy and compassion toward those in distress, and also of the desire to help or alleviate the pain or misery of those being hurt or maltreated, even to the point of torture. . . . This atrophy leaves scar tissue in the form of a hardness, an intense selfishness, even mercilessness, proportionate to the amount of exposure and its play on the native temperament of each child.[27]

While the charges that Preston brought against children's radio programs were exceptionally severe and far-flung, her attack followed the pattern that had been established by the earlier critics of these programs. Like her predecessors, she attempted to see causal connections between those aspects of child behavior that she found disturbing and children's radio programs. The main difference between her and the other critics was that she provided rationalizations for even the most tenuous connections, whereas her fellow critics exercised a bit more caution in their accusations.

Another "professional" who criticized children's radio programs was Justice Jacob Panken, a prominent figure in New York's juvenile court system. In words that were reminiscent of Comstock's, Panken publicly condemned all children's programs that dealt with crime. Although these shows invariably portrayed criminals in a negative light, Panken maintained that crime programs encouraged children to become juvenile delinquents. During a conference on crime prevention held in April 1938, Panken elaborated on his objections to this type of programming. These shows, he asserted, "shocked" the young listener by overemphasizing the "ugly and vicious" aspects of society. Panken added that "instead of being taught a moral lesson," the child's "imagination is excited and an immoral attitude is the result."[28] It is noteworthy, however, that Panken was one of the few critics of children's radio programs who resorted to this Comstock-like line of reasoning.

In response to the increasing criticisms of their children's programs during the late 1930s, the networks began making changes in their programming schedules. They refused to ban all controversial programs from the airwaves, but they did try to appease their critics by broadcasting a few "educational" programs for children. In 1938, MBS hired Dorothy Gordon, a long-time critic of violent programs, to read classic children's stories over the air.[29] The following year CBS introduced Nila Mack's program, "Let's Pretend." Mack based her show on fairy tales, but she was careful to omit scenes from the tales that, in her opinion, were too frightening or gruesome.[30] Other educational shows included "Wilderness Road," "Singing Lady," and "Children's Corner." Although these programs won praise from such groups as the Women's National Radio Committee, the United Parents' Association, and the American Library Association, they had difficulty attracting large audiences or commerical sponsors.[31]

The networks failed to defuse the unfavorable publicity that surrounded the bulk of their children's programs by airing a few noncontroversial shows. This situation led a number of broadcasters to believe that the government was likely to begin interfering with their programming policies unless they made some significant changes. Hoping to avoid further regulation of their programming, the leaders of the National Association of Broadcasters decided that the association's members should adhere to a broadcasting code of ethics. The code was drawn up, and in July 1939 the membership voted to accept it.[32] It established standards for all children's programs:

> These programs should reflect respect for parents, adult authority, law and order, clean living, high morals, fair play and honorable behavior. Such programs must not contain sequences involving horror or torture or use of the supernatural or superstitious or any other material which might reasonably be regarded as likely to over-stimulate the child-listener, or be prejudicial to sound character development.[33]

Although the broadcasters' code of ethics was well publicized, it was only part of a larger strategy to deflate the controversy surrounding children's programming. Several broadcasters concluded that the most effective method of dealing with criticisms of their children's programs was simply to replace these shows with programs for adults. Thus, from 1938 to 1941, the networks gradually and quietly reduced the amount of time that they devoted to children's programs. CBS, for example, replaced almost all of its children's programs with soap operas.[34] For the most part, this tactic worked. Dorothy Gordon, one of the few people to voice strong objections to the reduction in children's programming, accused the networks of neglecting children in her 1942 book *All Children Listen*. Most of her potential allies, though, were too engrossed with the war effort to pay much attention to her charges.

Concern over the portrayal of violence on children's radio programs diminished during the war years. It may be that few reformers saw any point in protesting make-believe violence while the world was engulfed in its most violent war. Network executives and program sponsors responded to this development by airing several new adventure programs for children, including "Don Winslow of the Navy," "Hop Harrigan," and "Captain Midnight." These programs generally dealt with the war-time exploits of patriotic Americans, often featuring dog fights, bombing runs, prison escapes, and machine-gun battles.[35]

Shortly after the war ended, children's radio programs again came under attack. The National Council for Youth Entertainment, an organization formed in 1947, collected 350,000 signatures on a petition demanding that the networks stop broadcasting violent children's programs.[36] This post-war protest movement, however, proved to be unnecessary since children's radio shows, along with all other forms of radio programming, had been replaced by the comic book as the most controversial form of American children's culture.

The reformers who objected to children's radio programs during the 1930s and '40s and the children's librarians who campaigned against series books during the 1910s and '20s viewed children in a similar way. Both tended to think of childhood as a time of happiness and contentment. The critics of children's radio programs, however, more clearly defined their conception of childhood. They not only accused children's radio programs of spoiling children's natural happiness, but they also attributed specific emotional reactions to radio listening. Nightmares, fingernail biting, nervousness, and other signs of childhood anxieties and fears were all said to have been caused by the excitement and violence contained in children's programming. In the process of making this argument, these critics implied that normal children would not have any anxieties and fears if they were sheltered from "dangerous" radio programming. Children were now seen as psychologically fragile, not just corruptible. Since this notion had seldom been articulated before the 1930s, it represented the addition of a new dimension to the myth of childhood innocence.

While the critics of children's radio programs attempted to buttress their arguments with psychological theories and terminology, there can be little doubt that their belief that normal children do not have anxieties and fears was the product of wishful thinking rather than scientific research on child psychology. Nevertheless, the increased interest in child psychology among middle-class parents from the 1930s and '40s did affect their reactions to children's radio programs. Before this period, parents generally did not pay much attention to their children's psychological development. Certainly the child-rearing manuals that were published before the 1930s emphasized children's physical, intellectual, and moral growth over their psychological development. With the popularization of child psychology, however, some parents began to worry about their children's psychological and emotional well-being. If their children showed signs of being anxious, unhappy, or maladjusted, they became quite concerned. Indeed, such signs may have caused some parents to feel insecure about their child-rearing abilities. In an attempt to cope with these insecurities, some parents and certain reformers cast about for a scapegoat upon which they could blame all of their children's psychological problems. The nature of the charges that were brought against children's radio programming suggests that this form of culture functioned as this scapegoat. In this regard, the campaign against children's radio programs was similar to earlier controversies in American children's culture. Dime novels provided a convenient explanation for juvenile delinquency, and series books were singled out as the cause of childhood unhappiness and discontent. Thus, while dime novels, series books, and children's radio programs met with somewhat different criticisms, all three served as scapegoats.

5.

Fredric Wertham and
the Comic Book Controversy

Although a number of twentieth-century adults opposed the
portrayal of violence in children's culture, only a few devoted as
much time and energy exclusively to their campaigns as Anthony
Comstock dedicated to his battle against dime novels. Of these,
Fredric Wertham, the leading critic of comic books, came closest
to matching Comstock's crusading spirit. Wertham not only
shared his predecessor's tendencies toward zealotry, but he also
resurrected many of the arguments that Comstock had made
during the dime-novel controversy.

Despite their similarities, however, these men came from
radically different backgrounds. Comstock was a right-wing,
evangelical anti-intellectual, whereas Wertham was a liberal, non-
religious intellectual. Comstock had worked as a store clerk
before founding the New York Society for the Suppression of
Vice. Wertham, on the other hand, had training in psychiatry and
neurology and held prestigious positions in several universities
and hospitals, including Johns Hopkins Medical School, New
York University, and Bellevue Hospital. Thus, even though their
opinions on children's culture were often the same, Comstock
and Wertham approached this issue from drastically different
backgrounds.

Wertham's campaign against comic books grew out of his

interest in the causes of murder and brutality. Beginning in the early 1940s, Wertham became preoccupied with finding ways to prevent violence. Initially, he felt that the best solution to this problem was to provide psychiatric counseling for all people who performed or contemplated violent acts. He articulated this idea in *Dark Legend: A Study in Murder*, published in 1941, and elaborated on it in *The Show of Violence*, which came out in the spring of 1949. Wertham attempted to implement his idea by establishing the Lafargue Clinic in Harlem in March 1946. While the clinic provided low-cost, psychiatric counseling for anyone in the community, the staff members were especially interested in reaching troubled teenagers. As one of the social workers on the staff explained to a reporter, "We try to get them here while they're maladjusted and before they're delinquent. . . . [These teenagers] belong in psychiatric clinics, where we can give them treatment and a hope and direction."[1]

Wertham served as director of the Lafargue Clinic for many years, but he revised his thinking on violence a few years after the clinic opened. Rather than focus all of his attention on helping people control violent impulses, he decided to devote part of his time to uncovering the root causes of violent behavior. After studying several sociological reports that showed a correlation between violence and social conditions, he came to the conclusion that violent impulses are not an innate part of the human personality. By taking this position, he found himself in conflict with the Freudian assumption that all people possess feelings of aggression. He recognized this conflict and dealt with it by criticizing Freud. In an article published in the *Scientific American*, he argued that Freud's belief in the existence of a death instinct was related to Freud's depression over the "breakdown of the democratic transformation in Central Europe" during the 1920s and '30s. He dismissed Freud's theory that aggression is tied to the death instinct as dubious, and he argued that the psychoanalytic movement had gone "off the deep end" by accepting this theory. He concluded his article by accusing Freud and Freud's followers of "disregarding social realities" when accounting for human violence.[2]

The social forces that Wertham first cited as causing violent behavior were poverty and racism. In 1947, however, his interest in these causes of violence started to diminish after he began treating some of the Lafargue Clinic's younger clients. Over the course of his discussions with these children he discovered that reading comic books was one of their preferred pastimes. He was unfamiliar with these publications and asked to see some of these children's favorite comic books. He learned that many of these publications dealt with crime and violence. Since most of the children who showed their comic books to him had committed either criminal or violent acts, he concluded, to the considerable surprise of many of his fellow psychiatrists, that a causal relationship existed between reading comic books and juvenile delinquency. Convinced that he had discovered a major cause of violence, Wertham, together with several members of the staff of the Lafargue Clinic, began analyzing the contents of numerous comic books. Wertham focused this investigation on crime comic books. He included in this category all comics that featured detective stories as well as those that dealt with the violent adventures of superheroes.[3]

Although Wertham viewed the publication of these types of comic books as a recent phenomenon, they had in fact been in existence since the mid-1930s. *Detective Comics*, the earliest crime comic book, was first published by Harry Donenfeld in March 1937. Shortly after its appearance, *Action Comics* and *Police Comics* made their debuts. Superhero comic books began in 1938, when Jerry Siegel and Joe Shuster created the Superman character. A few years later a number of other comic books about superheroes appeared, including *Batman*, *Wonder Woman*, and *Captain Marvel*. In 1942, the comic book that Wertham detested most, *Crime Does Not Pay*, was brought out by Lev Gleason Publications. Thus, by the time Wertham started his investigation, comic books were already a well-established form of children's culture.[4]

After completing his preliminary investigation, Wertham launched his campaign against crime comic books. Early in 1948, he conducted a symposium on the psychopathology of comic books during a meeting of the Association for the Advancement of Psychotherapy, an organization over which he presided.[5] As a part of this symposium, he organized an exhibition of illustrations from dozens of comic books. In addition to informing his colleagues about his research, he also took his message to the general population. On 29 May 1948, the *Saturday Review of*

Literature published Wertham's first major article on comic books, and a few months later a condensed version of this article appeared in the *Reader's Digest.*

In the beginning of his article, Wertham used a tactic that Comstock had often employed to "prove" that dime novels bred criminals. Wertham described the actions of several young lawbreakers and then stated that these children also read crime comic books. On the basis of this evidence, he asserted:

> We are getting to the roots of one of the contributing causes of juvenile delinquency when we study the influence of comic books. You cannot understand present-day juvenile delinquency if you do not take into account the pathogenic and pathoplastic influence of comic books, that is, the way in which they cause trouble or determine the form that trouble takes.[6]

Although Wertham devoted most of his article to discussing the relationship between comic-book reading and violent behavior, he made reference to several other problems that he associated with comic books. These publications, he proclaimed, had immunized "a whole generation against pity and against recognition of cruelty and violence."[7] He also suggested that comic books stimulated "unhealthy sexual attitudes," but he neglected to explain exactly what he meant by this statement.[8] Perhaps his least controversial charge against comic books involved their pictorial nature. Since children could follow most comic books without reading the words, he argued that these publications did little to develop children's reading skills.[9] Soon after his article appeared, Wertham began lecturing about comic books. His lectures generally covered the same material that he presented in his article, but in some of them he made new accusations. In a speech that he delivered in June 1948, for example, he stated that "juvenile deliquency was increasing and growing in brutality," a phenomenon that he attributed to "comic books stressing crime, sex and sadism."[10] He was unable, however, to provide statistical evidence that supported his claim. Perhaps Wertham's most important speech on comic books was delivered at the 1948 Annual Congress of Correction, which was held in early September. Wertham told his audience that comic books were a form of "pollution" from which children needed to be protected. He then called for the passage of both federal and state laws that would prohibit the sale of comic books to children under fifteen years of age.[11]

Wertham's proposal to restrict the sale of comic books drew a considerable amount of attention. Dozens of newspapers published articles on Wertham's campaign, and leaders from several communities asked Wertham to help them draft local ordinances against comic books. As his visibility increased, however, his reputation among his colleagues began to diminish. Few psychiatrists or psychologists condoned Wertham's position on comic books, and a number of them publicly opposed his campaign. The decline in Wertham's professional standing was reflected in the articles that appeared in the *Journal of Educational Sociology* in December 1949. This issue dealt entirely with comic books and contained articles by several prominent psychologists, sociologists, and educators. Not one of these contributors agreed with Wertham's stand. Frederic M. Thrasher, for example, devoted his article, "The Comics and Delinquency: Cause or Scapegoat," to analyzing Wertham's research methods and scientific logic. Responding to Wertham's claim that comic books were a significant factor behind juvenile delinquency, Thrasher wrote:

This extreme position which is not substantiated by any valid research, is not only contrary to considerable current psychiatric thinking, but also disregards tested research procedures which have discredited numerous previous monistic theories of delinquency causation. Wertham's dark picture of the influence of comics is more forensic than it is scientific and illustrates a dangerous habit of projecting our social frustrations upon some specific trait of our culture, which becomes a sort of "whipping boy" for our failure to control the whole gamut of social breakdown.[12]

Wertham deeply resented his colleagues' criticisms of his campaign against comic books, and he rejected them outright. The defenders of comic books, he argued, lacked either common sense or compassion. His feelings of resentment caused him to distance himself from the psychiatric community. On numerous occasions, he accused his fellow psychiatrists of overemphasizing the importance of the id in the human personality. He also questioned their ability to cure patients. In 1950 he was asked if he thought psychoanalysis helped disturbed people, and he responded by saying that "eight out of ten psychoanalyses should not have been started and six out of ten were more harmful than helpful."[13]

The anger that Wertham felt toward his critics seems to have caused him to step up his campaign against the publishers of crime comic books. Not only did he continue attacking comic books in his articles and lectures, but he also began working for the passage of anti-comic-book laws. He helped write a Los Angeles County ordinance that banned young children from buying crime comic books, and he attempted to persuade post office officials that comic books should be treated as obscene publications.[14] In 1950 he convinced a number of New York state legislators that comic books posed a serious danger to the welfare of children. As a result, the Joint Legislative Committee to Study Comics was formed. The committee heard testimony from Wertham on two occasions. In December 1950, he asked the committee to support "a public health law which would forbid the sale and display of all crime comic books to children under the age of fifteen years."[15] One year later, he told the committee that comic books were "the cause of a psychological mutilation of children," and he again urged that his proposed law be enacted.[16] This time the committee agreed with Wertham. In March 1952, a bill making it a "misdemeanor to publish or sell comic books dealing with fictional crime, bloodshed or lust that might incite minors to violence or immorality" was approved by both the New York State Assembly and Senate.[17] The following month, however, Governor Thomas E. Dewey vetoed the bill on the grounds that its wording was so vague that it bordered on being unconstitutional.[18]

While Wertham was extremely disappointed over Dewey's veto, he refused to abandon his campaign. His experience with the New York legislators convinced him that the passage of anti-comic-book laws required the support of a large and vocal group of parents. With this idea in mind, he set out to convince the nation's parents that comic books undermined the moral development of their children. The best way to accomplish this goal, he determined, was to write an anti-comic-book manifesto, which

Wertham began writing in 1952 and continued working on during much of 1953. Some excerpts appeared in the *Ladies' Home Journal* in November 1953. A few months later the entire work was published as *Seduction of the Innocent*.

An air of sensationalism surrounded the publication of *Seduction of the Innocent*. It was advertised as "the most shocking book of the year,"[19] and its 397 pages were filled with the details of numerous crimes that young comic-book readers had allegedly committed. The general public, not the psychiatric community, was clearly the intended audience for this book. Wertham did not use the academic style that he employed in his more scholarly publications, and he made few references to the writings of other psychiatrists and psychologists on the causes of violent behavior. Like his articles on comic books, *Seduction of the Innocent* consisted primarily of his oft-repeated accusations and case reports. He did attempt, though, to provide his book with a theoretical foundation.

Wertham's theory on how comic books harmed their young readers was predicated on the old Lockean assumption that "hostility and destructiveness are . . . instilled in" children "from outside."[20] Comic books, according to Wertham, contributed to this process by introducing children to characters who possess these negative qualities. Wertham argued that children were led to view these characters as heroes and tended, therefore, to identify with them. Elaborating on this point, he wrote:

> In investigating the mechanism of identification in individual children with individual comic books, it became clear to me that comic books are conditioning children to identify themselves with the strong man, however evil he may be. The hero in crime comics is not the hero unless he acts like a criminal. And the criminal in comic books is not a criminal to the child because he acts like a hero. He lives like a hero until the very end, and even then he often dies like a hero, in a burst of gun-fire and violence.[21]

In Wertham's opinion, children who identified with comic-book heroes soon assimilated the negative traits that these characters exhibited. He argued that in the early stages of this corruptive process these children were likely to entertain "unwholesome fantasies" and "abnormal ideas."[22] As this process progressed, a number of these children were certain to act out some of their comic-book-inspired fantasies. Using this line of reasoning, Wertham not only associated comic books with juvenile deliquency, but he also attempted to establish a connection between these publications and homosexuality. After suggesting that the relationship between Batman and Robin had homoerotic overtones, Wertham warned parents that the "Batman type of story may stimulate children to homosexual fantasies."[23] Wertham also accused Wonder Woman of fostering homosexuality. He referred to this character as a lesbian, and argued that she frightened boy readers and set a "morbid ideal" for girls.[24]

Wertham realized that his theory minimized the role of parents in the formation of children's superegos. Throughout *Seduction of the Innocent*, he argued that comic books were capable of subverting the efforts of even the most conscientious parents. In fact, he concluded his book by stating that "the influence of a good home is frustrated if it is not supported by the other influences children are exposed to," by which he meant crime comic books.[25] In defending this position, Wertham claimed that many children were so impressed with the magnificent powers of Superman, Batman, Wonder Woman and the other comic-book heroes that they stopped admiring their own parents:

> How can . . . children respect the hard-working mother, father or teacher who is so pedestrian, trying to teach common rules of conduct, wanting you to keep your feet on the ground and unable even figuratively speaking to fly through the air? Psychologically Superman undermines the authority and dignity of the ordinary man and woman in minds of children.[26]

The publication of *Seduction of the Innocent* received much attention. Numerous periodicals, including the *Nation*, the *New Republic*, the *New York Times Book Review*, the *New Yorker*, and the *Saturday Review of Literature*, published lengthy reviews of it. *Commentary* devoted an entire article to the issues that Wertham discussed in his book and an excerpt from the book appeared in the *Reader's Digest* under the title "Comic Books, Blueprints for Delinquency." The book also attracted attention from parents' groups and women's organizations. A few of these groups were so moved by Wertham's arguments that they organized boycotts of businesses that sold crime comic books.[27] Much to Wertham's satisfaction, his book and the public's response to it convinced a powerful Senate liberal, Estes Kefauver of Tennessee, to investigate Wertham's charges against comic books. As a member of the Senate Subcommittee on Juvenile Delinquency, Kefauver asked Wertham to testify before the subcommittee.

Wertham presented his testimony on 24 April 1954. In his opening remarks, he stated that comic books were "an important contributing factor in many cases of juvenile delinquency."[28] He defended his position by advancing several arguments: the brutality portrayed in comic books caused children to experience "moral and ethical confusion"; the crimes depicted in comic books taught children various techniques of committing criminal acts; and the advertisements for acne medicines, weight-reducing products, and muscle-building plans that appeared in many comic books gave children "all kinds of inferiority feelings" which led them to engage in antisocial behavior.[29] Wertham concluded his testimony by renewing his call for a law that would prohibit children under fifteen from buying crime comic books.

Apparently impressed by Wertham's testimony, Kefauver and the other members of the subcommittee continued their investigation of the comic-book industry. They summoned a number of other witnesses to appear before them, including William M. Gaines, who published comic books, and William Richter, a representative of the Newsdealers Association of Greater New York.[30] Although the federal government never took any action against the comic-book industry, the publicity surrounding the subcommittee's hearings created the impression in the minds of many comic-book publishers that Wertham's proposed legislation might be passed.

These publishers reacted to the threat of impending legislative action against their industry by agreeing to adopt a program of self-regulation. In September 1954, the Comics Magazine Association of America, an organization representing twenty-four of the twenty-seven major publishers in the field, announced plans to adhere to a code of ethics, which was adopted the following month.[31] Like the codes that broadcasters had drawn up in response to criticisms of children's radio programs, this code prohibited the glorification of criminals and the depiction of all scenes of horror.[32] Judge Charles F. Murphy, an expert in matters relating to juvenile delinquency, was hired to enforce the code. Comic books that met with Murphy's approval bore a seal which read "Approved by the Comics Code Authority."[33] This system succeeded in both reducing the amount of violence portrayed in comic books and in defusing much of the controversy that surrounded the comic-book industry.

Claiming that the Comics Code was inadequate, Wertham refused to stop criticizing comic books. However, following the implementation of the comic-book industry's system of self-censorship, Wertham's campaign lost much of its momentum. During the second half of the 1950s, the news media tended to ignore his charges, and government officials seldom asked for his opinion on comic books. Although Wertham never abandoned his campaign, he did make some revisions in his assessment of the role that comic books played in children's lives, eventually concluding that violent television programs posed a greater danger to the welfare of children than did comic books.

Because he was unable to convince legislators that children should be prohibited legally from purchasing violent comic books, Wertham felt that his campaign was a failure. In many ways, though, it was a remarkable success. He managed, with little outside help, to persuade large numbers of parents, government officials, editors, and other adults that comic books harmed children, and he nearly succeeded in bringing about the passage of an anti-comic-book law in New York. Largely because of his efforts, the publishers whom he attacked felt compelled to adopt one of the most stringent codes of self-regulations in the history of twentieth-century American communications media. Finally, although he did not know it at the time, he helped lay the groundwork for future campaigns against children's television programs. Wertham's success stemmed, in part, from his ability to combine the moral fervor that Comstock had brought to his crusade against dime novels with the psychological theories and terminology that the critics of children's radio programs had used. This ability enabled Wertham to give the appearance of being both a passionate defender of innocent children and an objective expert on the causes of violent behavior.

Although Wertham was disappointed in the various national and state legislators who did not work for the passage of anti-comic-book laws, he felt especially bitter toward the many psy-chiatrists and psychologists who refused to support his campaign. He often complained that a vast chasm separated him from the rest of the psychiatric community. On occasion, he tried to bridge the gap but without much success. In November 1955, for exam-ple, he sent a letter to Karl Menninger, a well-known psychiatrist and cofounder of the Menninger Foundation, in which he asked Menninger for his support. "It would be nice," he wrote, "if you would write on the harm that violence in mass media can do; since so many psychiatrists who do not believe that now would be instructed by you."[34] Menninger, however, politely denied the request.

One of the main reasons why Wertham felt so isolated from his colleagues was that his views on childhood differed consider-ably from theirs. Wertham firmly believed in the idea of childhood innocence, whereas most other psychiatrists from the 1940s and '50s took a more Freudian view of childhood. During this period, numerous Freudian child psychiatrists and psychologists, includ-ing Bruno Bettelheim, Erik Erikson, Selma Fraiberg, Anna Freud, and Melanie Klein, rose to prominence. Although they did not always agree on how adults should react to children's aggressive and sexual behavior, they all felt that such behavior should not be interpreted as being unnatural.[35]

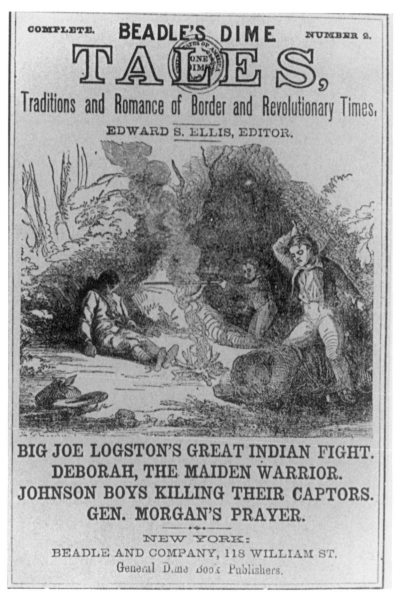

Cover of an early typical dime novel, 1863.

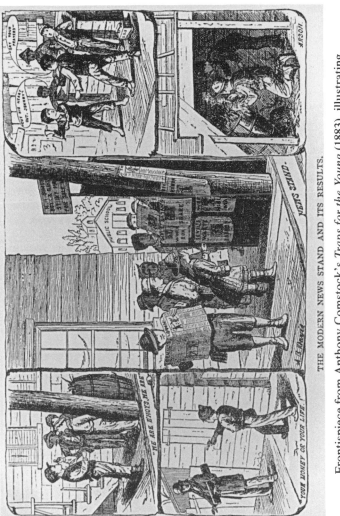

THE MODERN NEWS STAND AND ITS RESULTS.

Frontispiece from Anthony Comstock's *Traps for the Young* (1883), illustrating the pernicious effects of dime novels.

Cover of a half-dime novel, 1890.

Portrait of Anthony Comstock, the leading crusader for
moral purity. Frontispiece from Charles Gallaudet Trumbull's
biography, *Anthony Comstock, Fighter,* 1913.

THE CHILDREN'S RADIO HOUR

Cartoon depicting the proliferation of violent children's radio programs. *Parents' Magazine*, May 1933.

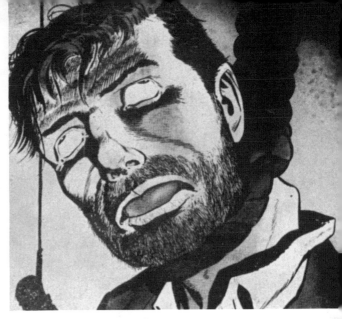

"Gruesome" comic book panel reprinted by Fredric Wertham in his *Seduction of the Innocent* (1954).

"Pornographic" comic book panel reprinted by Fredric Wertham in his *Seduction of the Innocent* (1954). *below*

Publicity still from *The Moon is Blue,* the film at the center of the Kansas State Boa~~of Review~~ censorship controversy from 1953 to 1955. Courtesy United Artists/ Kobal Collection.

Elvis Presley performing at 1956 Mississippi-Alabama state fair. AP/Wide World Photos.

Bestselling children's author Judy Blume, one of the leading "New Realists." Photo by George Cooper.

Bestselling children's author Norma Klein, one of the leading "New Realists." Photo by Thomas Victor.

6.

Film Censorship, Sexuality, and the Youth of Kansas

Fredric Wertham's belief that state government should become involved in the censorship of comic books was not without precedent. Soon after the birth of motion pictures, a number of states started censoring them. By 1915, Kansas, Pennsylvania, and Ohio had already begun censoring films, and not long thereafter Maryland, New York, Massachusetts, Virginia, and Louisiana followed suit.[1] Among the various state agencies that censored films, the Kansas State Board of Review was one of the most vigorous as well as one of the longest lived. Although it began losing power in the early 1950s, it continued to function until 1966.

Throughout its long history, the Kansas State Board of Review justified its existence on the grounds that it helped preserve the moral integrity of the state's children by sheltering them from films that dealt with sexuality and other "immoral" subjects. This line of reasoning went unquestioned for decades until the early 1950s, when it came under legal challenge. At the same time that psychiatrists were reexamining the myth of childhood innocence, the courts began rejecting the argument that children must be sheltered from all references to sexuality. In two crucial cases, the courts ruled against the board, and in so doing they undermined the board's authority and helped legitimize the idea that sexuality is a natural aspect of childhood.

54

Kansas passed a law that called for the censorship of films in 1913, but the state did not start censoring them until 12 April 1915. The State Superintendent of Public Instruction, W. D. Ross, served as the state's first film censor. Ross and his two assistants banned any film that, in their opinion, threatened "public morals." They censored a film entitled *Madame La Presidente*, for example, because it showed a man flirting with a married woman, and they banned several films because they contained "scenes of drunkenness." They also refused to allow *Birth of a Nation* to be shown because they felt it excited racial prejudice. This decision sparked a major controversy and caused some people to question the validity of the state's censorship law. In part because of this controversy, a more clearly defined censorship law was passed in 1917.[2] The new statute empowered the state to censor films that were deemed "cruel, obscene, indecent, or immoral, or such as tend to debase or corrupt morals."[3]

The responsibility of censoring films was entrusted to a three-member board called the Kansas State Board of Review. The law stipulated that the governor appoint each member of the board to a three-year term which could be renewed. Anyone wishing to show a film in Kansas had to submit it to the board for approval. The law also required the board to charge a small fee for each film it reviewed, thereby generating the funds necessary to pay the board members' salaries and expenses. In selecting the board's first members, Governor Arthur Capper decided to consider only women for the positions. Practically every governor after Capper continued this tradition even though the law did not require them to do so.

Soon after the appointment of the first board, the members adopted a set of guidelines that remained in effect for many years. In addition to demanding that "pictures should be clean and wholesome," these guidelines called for the censorship of all films that ridiculed religious or racial groups, that dealt with "infidelity to marriage ties" or "crimes and deeds of violence," or that contained "nude human figures," "bar-room scenes" or "prolonged passionate love scenes."[4] In establishing these guidelines, the board felt that it was helping to prevent the youth of Kansas from becoming depraved criminals. The board stressed this point in its first annual report which it submitted to Governor Capper in July 1918:

A majority of the films presented for censorship deal directly with crime, depicting all possible phases of it, and when we consider that these films do not reach adult audiences exclusively but that children of all ages view them, the disastrous effects upon young and plastic minds are readily seen. The strongest possible impression made upon these young minds comes through the eyes. Thus greater damage is being done to the children and youth of our land by bad pictures, than ever came from the cheap yellow-back literature of the Nick Carter variety a generation ago.[5]

During the 1920s, the board acted with great vigor. It eliminated scenes from approximately six hundred films each year and completely prohibited many other films from being shown in the state.[6] Some of the other states that censored films were equally zealous during this decade. This trend alarmed many film producers, some of whom feared that it would eventually lead to federal censorship. In an attempt to head off that possibility, a number of prominent figures in the film industry began to take countermeasures. In 1922, these people formed the Motion Picture Producers and Distributors Association and named Will H. Hays as the organization's president. Hays and his supporters felt that the best way to fight governmental censorship was to adopt a program of self-censorship. After several false starts, Hays succeeded in convincing the major film producers to adhere to a uniform set of standards known as the Motion Picture Production Code. This code took effect in 1930, and soon thereafter the demands for governmental censorship of films began to diminish.[7]

With the advent of the Production Code, the Kansas State Board of Review found that it no longer had so many objections to Hollywood's creations. The board, however, continued to function throughout the 1930s and '40s. During this period, the board attracted little attention, but its power actually increased. In 1931, the Kansas Federation of Business and Professional Women's Clubs spearheaded a drive to empower the board to censor the soundtracks of films. Claiming that "many 'talkie' pictures contain spoken lines that are debasing and tend to give young girls the wrong impressions of life and social contacts,"[8] the leaders of these clubs convinced the Kansas legislature to amend the censorship law so that the board could censor spoken dialogue as well. Another development that occurred in the 1930s came about after the board screened an educational film entitled *The Birth of a Baby*. The board members decided to ban the film but discovered that their guidelines said nothing about childbirth. In order to protect themselves, the board held a special meeting on 28 April 1939 to pass the following motion: "Ridicule or facetious remarks about motherhood, or, scenes pertaining to child-birth will be disapproved."[9] However, even though the board's authority increased, the number of films that the board altered or banned per year gradually diminished. In the 1940s, the board actively censored only thirty films during a typical year, which is about one twentieth the number it had censored each year of the 1920s.[10]

At the same time that the board was decreasing the number of films that it censored, it also began to interpret its guidelines more narrowly. The board remained adamantly opposed to the depiction of sexuality or anything related to sexuality, but films containing controversial political and religious statements got through the board's review process without being censored. The board also began to ignore scenes portraying drunkenness or violence. Although this change occurred gradually, two events helped push the board in this direction. In 1937, it censored a newsreel in which Senator Burton K. Wheeler, a Republican from Montana, criticized President Roosevelt's appointments to the Supreme Court. The board justified its actions on the grounds that Wheeler's remarks were biased, but Wheeler and many of his fellow Republicans strongly objected. At the insistence of Governor Walter Huxman, a Democrat, the board rescinded its decision and afterwards was much more cautious when censoring the views of political figures.[11] The board became even more cautious following a United States Supreme Court decision in 1952. The Court ruled that New York State had exceeded its legal bounds when it censored the film *The Miracle* for being sacrilegious.[12] Although this decision did not specifically address the censorship law in Kansas, it worried the board's chair, Frances Vaughn. At her request, Harold Fatzer, the attorney general of Kansas, examined the Kansas statutes dealing with film censorship to determine their constitutionality. In his letter to Vaughn, he stated that so long as the board limited itself to censoring "obscene" films it need not fear legal action.[13]

Vaughn and the other members of the board attempted to follow Fatzer's advice, but they did not succeed in avoiding legal action. Less than a year after the Supreme Court prohibited New York from banning *The Miracle*, Vaughn and her colleagues found themselves in one of the most serious court cases in the board's history. The origins of this case can be traced back to June 1953, for it was during this month that the board members viewed Otto Preminger's *The Moon is Blue*, a romantic comedy based on a play by F. Hugh Herbert. Although the film contains no profanity or scenes of sexual encounters, it uses sexually related words such as "virgin," "seduce," "pregnant," "mistress," and "aphrodisiac." The board members felt that children should not be allowed to hear such language. They also objected to the film because it refers to adultery and it features a young woman who is openly curious about sexual matters. For these reasons, they decided not to allow the film to be shown. As they did for each film that they banned, they jotted down their objections to the film on the back of a file card. In this case, the card read, "Sex theme throughout, too frank bedroom dialogue: many sexy words; both dialogue and action have sex as their theme."[14]

The board members did not expect that their decision would spark much controversy because their position was roughly the same as that taken by Joseph Breen, the administrator in charge of enforcing the Production Code throughout the 1940s and early '50s. Breen refused to grant the film the Production Code seal unless Preminger deleted several sexually related words and phrases from the script. Preminger, however, refused to comply and, instead, made and distributed the film without the seal, making him the first major American filmmaker to defy the Production Code since its implementation.[15] This same spirit of defiance surfaced again when Preminger learned that his film had been banned in Kansas.

A few days after the board decided to ban *The Moon is Blue*, a representative of Holmby Productions, Preminger's production company, met with Vaughn and offered to distribute the film only to those theaters that would agree not to allow children to see it. Since the board members had said that they banned the film in order to protect children, this proposal appeared to alleviate their concerns. Vaughn, however, did not see it this way. In her mind, accepting this proposal could potentially lead to the board's dissolution, for, as she often argued, protecting children was the board's raison d'etre. She therefore turned down the proposal. Soon after the meeting, she wrote a letter to the attorney general in which she told him of the proposal and asked him if he would support the decision.[16] He assured her that the statutes made no provisions "for a qualified or conditional approval based upon a agreement by the distributor to permit the film to be shown to adults only."[17] Relieved, Vaughn hoped that she had heard the last from Holmby Productions; but she had not.

Once it became clear that the board was not going to accept their compromise proposal, Holmby Productions and United Artists, the distributor of *The Moon is Blue*, decided to sue the board in an attempt to test the constitutionality of the state's statutes dealing with film censorship. Faced with its first lawsuit in many years, the board hired Arthur J. Stanley, Jr., a Kansas City lawyer, to serve as its legal counsel. Upon reviewing the case, Stanley realized that the original reasons that the board gave for banning the film could be interpreted as being arbitrary. Consequently, he sent a letter to Vaughn, advising her to re-examine the film and then send Holmby Productions "another letter of disapproval which would follow the words of the statute." In an effort to augment the board's defense, he went on to offer some additional advice:

> I would then suggest that you invite the Juvenile Judge of Wyandotte County, the head of the Family Welfare Service, and representatives of the Police Department Youth Bureau and the City Welfare Department to attend the showing of the film so that they would be available as witnesses as to the probable effect of the film on children who might see it at neighborhood theaters.[18]

Heeding Stanley's advice, the board members re-examined the film on 11 September 1953. As expected, they once again disapproved it, but this time they said that they "found the film to be obscene, indecent and immoral and such as tend to debase or corrupt morals."[19] Stanley felt more comfortable with this new wording because it emphasized the word "obscene," and he intended to base the board's defense on the state's right to censor obscenity. In writing the brief for the defendants, Stanley cited several cases in which the courts had upheld the constitutionality of censoring obscene material, and he attempted to use these cases to show that the Kansas censorship law was constitutional. Stanley realized, of course, that this approach required that he define obscenity in such a way that it would encompass *The Moon is Blue*, a film with no sexually explicit scenes. He attempted to solve this problem by defining as obscene anything that could threaten childhood innocence. After summarizing several earlier attempts to define the word, he concluded his argument by stating his definition of obscenity and then applying it to the film:

> The Court will have noticed that, running through the definitions of the word "obscene" . . . is the thought that the book, the article or the picture in question has a tendency to implant in the minds of the young, or others easily influenced, lewd or lascivious thoughts or desires. Certainly the same definition would be applicable to motion pictures.
>
> Plaintiffs have asserted that the words "pregnant," "seduce," "virgin" and "mistress" are words which would not be avoided in ordinary speech. Perhaps this is true, as far as sophisticated adults are concerned, but we doubt that able counsel for the plaintiffs would themselves use such words in ordinary conversation with children of high school age and we are of the opinion that counsel would be surprised and shocked if they should overhear teen-agers using these words or the words "aphrodisiac" or "yohimbine."
>
> The words "obscene" and "indecent" are words capable of accurate application and are not so vague as to make the statute invalid.[20]

Although Holmby Productions filed suit in Wyandotte County District Court in the fall of 1953, the case was not heard until July 1954. Judge Harry G. Miller ruled against the board, and in so doing he essentially invalidated the state statute dealing with film censorship. The statute, he argued, was so vaguely worded that it infringed on constitutional rights.[21] The board appealed the case to the Kansas Supreme Court, but before the case could be heard, the Kansas legislature nearly disbanded the board. In the wake of Miller's decision, the legislature passed a bill that repealed the censorship law, and Governor Fred Hall signed it on 7 April 1955.[22] Two days after Hall signed the bill, the Kansas Supreme Court overruled Miller's decision, but few people expressed much concern since at that point the board was scheduled to be abolished on 30 June 1955.[23] It was soon discovered, however, that the legislature had made a technical error when it passed the bill repealing the censorship law. Thus, in June 1955, the Kansas Supreme Court ruled the bill invalid. This meant that the board continued to function, and its ban on *The Moon is Blue* remained in effect.[24]

Undaunted by this bewildering series of events, Holmby Productions and United Artists appealed their case to the United States Supreme Court. On 24 October 1955, the Supreme Court reversed the decision of the Kansas Supreme Court and ruled that *The Moon is Blue* could not be banned for being "obscene."[25] In announcing its ruling, the Supreme Court cited *The Miracle* decision as well as another decision dealing with film censorship. But it issued no opinion along with its decision, and this resulted in some confusion about the decision's implications. Some interpreted the decision as a sign that the Supreme Court disapproved of the Kansas censorship law, while others argued that the decision simply meant that the Supreme Court disapproved of the board's interpretation of the law.[26] In either case, it was clear that the Supreme Court did not agree with the defendants' argument that any form of culture which threatened childhood innocence could be termed obscene. Although this decision did not end film censorship in Kansas, it forced the board to take a narrower view of obscenity. The decision also meant that all Kansans, including minors, could finally see *The Moon is Blue* in their neighborhood theaters.

The events of 1955 left the board shaken. The members knew that the board's future was uncertain, and they were no longer sure how to interpret the guidelines that the board had been working under since its inception. They also felt anger toward the governor for not backing them when the legislature attempted to abolish the board. Because of these factors, Vaughn resigned as chair of the board on 18 January 1956, saying that she saw "no percentage in staying on and trying to hold a semblance of order in the chaos.''[27] She was replaced by Mary Cook, who soon found herself fighting off another attempt to disband the board.

In March 1957, Bill 334 was introduced before the Kansas legislature, proposing to abolish the board and replace it with a series of penalties for exhibiting obscene films. Backers of the bill argued that it was fairer than the original censorship law because it did not involve prior censorship. Cook spoke out against the bill in speeches as well as in letters to lawmakers.[28] Like her predecessors, she argued that abolishing the board would harm children. She emphasized this point in a letter to the chair of the House Affairs Committee:

> I hope you will vote against house Bill 334, as I believe there is more need for the motion picture censor Board now than ever before. There is quite a little pressure being brought on us to pass pictures of obscene and immoral nature. . . . Only today we refused to pass a picture entitled, *The Story of Bob and Sallie.* . . . We refused to pass this picture as it had a low moral theme throughout—too sexy, intimate relations, child birth, also the function of both male and female sex organs, also nudity. . . . It was very embarrassing to watch and I think that you and your committee will agree such pictures as these are not fit for public showing, especially for young folks to see.[29]

Cook's argument apparently had its desired effect, for the bill was defeated by a vote of 54 to 68.[30] This was one of the last times that the board succeeded in winning support by describing itself as a protector of children.

In December 1957, the board's next legal battle began. This time the conflict focused on a film entitled *Mom and Dad.* First released in 1948, the film combines lessons on reproduction, contraception, childbirth, and venereal disease with a simple story about a young woman who accidentally becomes pregnant. Toward the end of the film, two childbirth scenes are shown. In one scene the child is born in the conventional way, while the other shows a cesarean section.[31] A revised version of the film was released in 1957, and the distributor, Capitol Enterprises, submitted it to the board for review even though the board had already banned the original version of the film. Around the same time that the film arrived at the board's office, Cook received a letter from Ephraim S. London, an attorney for Capitol Enterprises, hinting at a possible lawsuit if the board rejected the film. London made it clear that he and the distributor were well aware of the board's regulation against birth scenes, but, he went on to add, "we do not think that regulation is valid."[32]

London's confidence stemmed, in part, from a Supreme Court ruling known as the Roth decision. The case came about after Samuel Roth, a New York publisher of sexually oriented books and magazines, was convicted of violating a federal law which prohibited the mailing of obscene materials. Roth appealed his conviction to the Supreme Court on the grounds that the postal obscenity laws were too vague. The Supreme Court heard the case in April 1957 and upheld Roth's conviction. In writing the opinion, however, Justice William J. Brennan stated that "sex and obscenity are not synonymous." He then asserted that material could be classified as obscene only if an "average person, applying contemporary community standards," believed that "the dominant theme of the material taken as a whole appeals to prurient interest."[33] Given this definition of obscenity, London felt that *Mom and Dad* could not be called obscene and was therefore protected by the First Amendment.

Cook, of course, knew of the Roth decision, but she and her fellow board members held to their conviction that the childbirth scenes in *Mom and Dad* were obscene. On 2 January 1958, Cook notified London that the board members refused to pass the film because they did not consider it "proper for showing for entertainment."[34] Since Cook realized that this decision would spark a confrontation, she immediately began seeking the support of political and community leaders. The same day she wrote to London, she sent a letter to Senator August Lauterbac in which she referred to the childbirth scenes in the film and asked, "Do you honestly think such pictures are proper for theatres where people, young and old, go for entertainment?"[35] Such lobbying efforts, however, did little to help the board in its showdown with Capitol Enterprises.

In the early stages of this confrontation, both sides changed their key players. Cook stepped down as chair, and Hazel Runyan took her place. At the same time, the executives at Capitol

Enterprises hired Harold H. Harding, a Kansas City lawyer, to represent their interests. Throughout April and May 1958, Runyan and Harding exchanged a series of letters in which some possible compromises were discussed. Runyan offered to pass the film if Capitol Enterprises eliminated the "actual birth scenes" and the "scenes pertaining to conception."[36] Harding said that the company was willing to take out the information about conception but would not agree "to the cutting or deletion of the sequences dealing with the actual birth of a child."[37] Since they were unable to reach an agreement, Harding filed suit in Wyandotte County District Court.

In February 1959, the case was argued before Judge O. Q. Claflin, III. The attorneys for the board restated their argument that the film was obscene because it contained sexually related material that could harm child viewers, while the attorneys for Capitol Enterprises argued that the board's decision to ban the film was based on an unconstitutional definition of obscenity. In a ruling issued on 5 March 1959, Claflin decided against the board. Referring to several Supreme Court decisions, he determined that the film was "not obscene," and ordered the board to grant Capitol Enterprises "a certificate of approval for the exhibition throughout the state of Kansas of the motion picture film *Mom and Dad.*"[38]

Claflin's decision dramatically curtailed the board's power. The board was forced to abandon its previous criteria for censoring films and replace them with a narrowly worded regulation that was modeled after the guidelines set forth in the Roth decision. Though considerably weakened, the board continued to function until 1966 when the Kansas Supreme Court struck down the state's censorship law on the grounds that it violated "the constitutional guaranty of freedom of expression."[39] On 1 August 1966, a few days after the court announced its decision, Governor William Avery wrote to the board's chair, informing her that the board had sixty days to terminate its affairs and dispose of its property,[40] thus concluding the turbulent history of the Kansas State Board of Review.

The board's demise reflected Americans' growing distaste for censorship. On another level, though, it also marked a major shift in Americans' attitudes toward childhood sexuality. In the years before World War II, few questioned the board's insistence on sheltering children from all references to sexuality. Many Americans from this period tried to deny the existence of childhood sexuality, and they generally felt that children should not be exposed to information about sexuality. In the 1940s, however, this attitude started to give way to a more tolerant view of childhood sexuality. Prominent child-care experts, such as Benjamin Spock, argued that children have a natural interest in sexuality, and many parents were beginning to agree with this argument. This growing acceptance of childhood sexuality conflicted with the board's stand against *The Moon is Blue* and *Mom and Dad*. For increasing numbers of Americans, the sexual references in these films were seen as posing little danger to their children's well-being. Thus, when the courts overruled the board's right to censor these films, there was little public outcry. In a sense, the courts' decisions on these films simply gave legal credence to a view of childhood that had already gained a large following among educated, middle-class Americans.

7.

Elvis Presley, Jimmy Snow, and the Controversy Over Rock 'n' Roll

In tracing the evolution of Americans' attitudes toward the sexuality of young people, the 1950s stand out as an important turning point. Prior to this time, discussions of childhood sexuality were primarily confined to "professional" circles. Psychologists and psychiatrists debated the issue, as did lawyers and judges, but the general public tended to remain silent on the subject. This silence, however, became increasingly difficult to maintain in the face of the prolongation of childhood into the teenage years. While the idea that adolescence be viewed as an extension of childhood had been articulated early in the twentieth century, it was not until after World War II that it won widespread acceptance. As a result, the teenagers of the 1950s generally stayed in school until they were seventeen or eighteen, and so long as they remained in school they tended to be treated as children. But at these ages, it was impossible to pretend teenagers were not interested in sex. They were, even though they knew that society now expected them to put off marriage until they had graduated from high school. One of the ways in which their interest in sexuality manifested itself was in the music they liked. They gravitated toward music that had a strong sexual undercurrent to it, and that music came to be known as rock 'n' roll. Thus, when rock 'n' roll burst on the scene in the mid-1950s, it helped bring the topic of childhood sexuality into the open.

Many adults began expressing concern over the impact of rock music on children's sexual development. Other issues also contributed to the uproar that greeted rock 'n' roll. As Linda Martin and Kerry Segrave point out in their book, *Anti-Rock*, some racists disliked the black origins of the music, and some well-established artists and executives in the recording industry felt threatened by this new phenomenon. On the whole, though, the most frequently voiced objections had to do with the sexual nature of rock 'n' roll.[1]

Many of the early rock 'n' roll songs were sexually charged. In some cases, the songs featured risque lyrics. This was especially true of many of the black groups' hits. Groups such as the Dominoes, the Drifters, and the Midnighters all made extensive use of double entendres as well as sexually related words and sounds. A number of white singers did the same thing, but often toning down the lyrics somewhat. Many rock 'n' rollers from this period relied on phrasing and intonation to underscore the sexual connotations of certain words. Jerry Lee Lewis, for example, drew heavily on this technique when he sang "Whole Lotta Shakin'." Other performers, such as Little Richard, conveyed sexual messages through the way they dressed and moved their bodies. Of all the early rock 'n' roll stars, however, none could match Elvis Presley's ability to communicate sexual messages through his music.

Even in the beginning stages of his singing career, Presley deliberately cultivated his sexual appeal. In July 1954, at one of his first public concerts, he discovered that the young women in the audience responded positively to his leg and hip movements.[2] Once he became aware of their response, he began to play up this aspect of his performance, and soon thereafter was dubbed "Elvis the Pelvis." In addition to gyrating his hips, Presley imitated the looks and behavior of Marlon Brando, Jimmy Dean, and some of the other male sex symbols of the day. His hairstyle, sideburns, and famous sneer were all part of an attempt to look like one of these Hollywood heroes.[3] Ultimately, however, much of his sexual appeal stemmed not from his onstage behavior and appearance, but from the sound of his music. Like most early rock 'n' roll, his songs had a strong, lively beat that almost demanded a physical response. He also had a knack for phrasing words in such a way that they resonated with sexual tension. As Albert Goldman, one of Presley's biographers, points out, this knack was evident in his first commercial record, "That's All Right," released in August 1954:

> Pitching his voice way up high, in a range that suggests ecstasy, Elvis phrases the lines so that they stretch and yearn and writhe like a boogaloo; then, when he reaches the refrain, "That's all right, mama, that's all right with me," he teases and taunts and releases the tension he has been building in a cadence that drifts down with sensuous little swells and diminuendos like a dancer boogeyin' down. The total effect can be summed up in one word—sexy![4]

Presley's brand of rock 'n' roll generated controversy from the very beginning, but during 1954 and '55 this controversy was fairly localized. Although his concerts occasionally came under attack, the protests tended to fade away as soon as he left town. Once Presley became a national celebrity, however, the attacks on his music and performance style escalated dramatically. Presley's critics seemed especially alarmed over the effects that his music had on the thousands of teenage girls who flocked to his concerts and purchased his records. These girls made it no secret that they enjoyed the sexual aspects of Presley's performance, causing a great deal of concern among those adults who thought that girls should not be interested in sex.

Presley's detractors launched their barrage in 1956 and kept it up through 1957. In some cases, they actually destroyed his records. An enterprising used-car dealer from Cincinnati offered to smash fifty of Presley's records for each car that he sold. On the first day of the offer, he had five takers.[5] In Nashville, a disgruntled disc jockey sponsored a public burning of Presley's records; when the flames finally died away, six hundred records had been reduced to a lump of molten vinyl.[6] Many of the attacks on Presley came from the pulpit. For example, the Reverend Charles Howard Graff of St. John's Episcopal Church in Greenwich Village denounced Presley as a "whirling dervish of sex."[7] Such name-calling typified most of the negative responses to

Presley, be they from religious figures, representatives of the news media, or ordinary members of the public. A few of his critics, however, attempted to explain why they objected to his music. Perhaps the most articulate of these was Jack Gould, the television critic for the *New York Times*.

Gould first set his sights on Presley on 6 June 1956. On the previous evening, Presley had appeared on "The Milton Berle Show," and Gould decided that this made Presley fair game for a television critic. He said that Presley had "no discernible singing ability" and went on to call him a "virtuoso of the hootchy-kootchy."[8] On 9 September 1956, Presley made his debut on Ed Sullivan's "Toast of the Town", and once again Gould responded with a salvo. This time Gould said that Presley's songs amounted to little more than "assaults on the American ear."[9] A few days later, Gould published his longest and most thoughtful piece on Presley. Putting into words what many other Presley detractors only implied, Gould argued that Presley and the television programs that featured Presley were harming the sexual development of teenagers:

> The teenager is susceptible to overstimulation from the outside. He is at an age when the awareness of sex is both thoroughly natural and normal, when latent rebellion is to be expected. But what is new and a little discouraging is the willingness and indeed eagerness of reputable businessmen to exploit these critical factors beyond all reasonable grounds.
>
> When Presley executes his bumps and grinds, it must be remembered by the Columbia Broadcasting System that even the twelve-year-old's curiosity may be overstimulated.
>
> The industry lives fundamentally by the code of giving the public what it wants. But when this code is applied to teenagers just becoming conscious of life's processes, not only is it manifestly without validity but also it is perilous. . . . Selfish exploitation and commercialized overstimulation of youth's physical impulses is certainly a gross national disservice.[10]

The controversy surrounding Presley diminished around the same time he was drafted into the army. Presley reported for duty on 20 March 1958, and for the next two years he took a hiatus from his singing career. Since he did not appear on television programs or perform at concerts, his critics were forced to limit their attacks to his records. As a result, their condemnations and dire warnings no longer seemed quite so urgent or newsworthy. The pictures of Presley in his uniform and the reports that he was an exemplary soldier further undermined his critics' accusations. Also during this period, his mother died, causing the public to sympathize with him. All of these factors worked against Presley's "bad boy" image and helped make him into a more acceptable figure among mainstream Americans.

Presley's growing respectability reflected an overall change in Americans' attitudes toward rock 'n' roll. As the 1950s came to a close, the initial shock waves that followed the sudden emergence of rock music were gradually subsiding. Although many adults continued to dislike rock 'n'roll, they were becoming more accustomed to hearing it on their car radios or coming from their children's bedrooms. The more familiar they became with it, the less threatening it sounded. They were also becoming more familiar with rock 'n' roll sex symbols. During this period, a host of singers, including Ricky Nelson, Fabian, Frankie Avalon, and Bobby Darin, discovered that by imitating Presley's singing style and body movements they, too, could win the hearts of teenage girls. Thus, Presley no longer seemed so exotic.[11]

Another phenomenon that Americans were learning to accept was the response of teenagers to rock 'n' roll. In the mid-1950s, the screaming and energetic dancing that usually occurred at rock concerts had often been described as rioting, but by the decade's end this term seldom appeared in descriptions of fan behavior. In the eyes of increasing numbers of adults, the antics of rock 'n' roll fans were seen not as dangerous, but as silly. Similarly, more and more parents came to accept their daughters' crushes on rock stars as just another one of the annoying phases that teenage girls went through. In other words, the growing toleration of rock 'n' roll was tied to a more accepting attitude toward teenagers' sexual fantasies.

When Presley returned to civilian life in March 1960, the controversy surrounding rock 'n' roll had largely disappeared. This development had a profound impact on his career. Instead of being viewed as a leader of a deviant form of entertainment, he was now seen as the head of a well-established branch of popular culture. With this change came a new title. The press began calling him the "King of Rock 'n' Roll" rather than "Elvis the Pelvis." Not everyone, however, was ready to make peace with rock 'n' roll or its newly dubbed king. Although they received little publicity, rock 'n' roll still had some ardent opponents. For the most part, these people lived in the South and had strong religious affiliations. While the rest of the nation welcomed back the "King," some of the opponents of rock 'n' roll turned their attention to a former friend of Presley's, a young man named Jimmy Rodgers Snow. Although Snow's attack on rock 'n' roll is a minor episode in the continuing battle against the music, it foreshadows the reactions of fundamentalist Christians to America's changing sexual mores.

Snow and Presley became acquainted in January 1955 when they appreared together at a concert in Lubbock, Texas. At the time, it was Snow, not Presley, who appeared to be on the verge of stardom. His father, country music star Hank Snow, had spent years grooming the young Snow for a career in show business. At his father's insistence, Jimmy Snow began singing for audiences as soon as he learned to talk and continued to be a part of his father's act throughout his childhood.[12] Thus, even though Snow was only nineteen in 1955, he already had many years of professional experience. Also, thanks to his father, he had no trouble finding work. Hank Snow, together with Colonel Thomas Parker, owned Hank Snow's Jamboree Attractions, a tour packaging agency, and they regularly booked Jimmy Snow on their tours. What Snow lacked, however, was Presley's drive and charisma, and this difference became apparent soon after the two began performing together.

The idea of pairing up Snow and Presley originated with Parker. As one of Nashville's leading music promoters, Parker had heard various reports about Presley's unique singing style, and he wanted to determine whether they were true. He made arrangements for the concert in Lubbock and instructed Snow to give him a full account of Presley's performance. Snow returned with a glowing report, and immediately afterward Parker decided to book Snow and Presley on a ten-day tour of the Southwest. Although the showbill listed Presley's name below Snow's, it soon became clear that Presley was the star of the show.[13] This, however, did not prevent the two young singers from becoming friends. As Snow later recalled in his autobiography, *I Cannot Go Back*, they got along well despite the fact that their personalities differed considerably:

> Elvis and I made a strange pair. He dressed like a dude, clowned and capered, and was the life of the party. I wore a straight cowboy suit and sat around trying to think of something to say. He didn't smoke, drink, or curse and sirred and ma'amed everybody over twenty-one. I had all the vices and wore a chip on my shoulder. But we both liked girls for sex and boys for company.[14]

Not long after they returned from their tour, Presley's career rapidly gathered momentum while Snow's gradually unraveled. During the next two years, Snow made a half hearted attempt to switch from country music rock 'n' roll. He toured again with Presley, worked a little with Bill Haley, and even released a rock 'n' roll single called "The Rules of Love." But his bursts of productivity came between long periods of inactivity. As he later admitted, he had serious problems with drugs and alcohol and lacked any self-discipline. These problems not only tarnished his reputation in the music industry, but they also led to a major conflict with his father. The senior Snow became so disgusted with his son that he disinherited him. After Jimmy Snow read the revised will that his father insisted on showing him, he felt overwhelmed with a sense of failure.[15]

One November evening in 1957, Snow decided to put an end to his problems. He loaded his revolver, placed the barrel in his mouth, and tried to make his finger pull the trigger. But his finger would not cooperate. Disgusted with himself, he ran out of the house and collapsed in front of his mailbox. There, according to Snow, God gave him a message. In recalling this event, Snow wrote, "God had not only accepted me; He was going to use me in His service. Like Moses, I was going to be His spokesman."[16] That very evening he visited the pastor of an Assembly of God church that he had occasionally attended with a former girlfriend. The pastor praised Snow's decision to become a preacher and encouraged him to go to Bible college that coming fall. Although this struck Snow as a good idea, the fall was months away, and he was not sure what to do in the meantime.

While Snow pondered his future, he received an invitation to visit Presley in Memphis. Snow accepted and spent the first ten days of 1958 with his former singing partner. Even though Presley treated Snow kindly, the visit proved to be a trying experience for Snow. As he wandered Graceland Mansion, rode in Presley's Cadillacs, and attended a private showing of Presley's third feature film, *Jailhouse Rock*, Snow could not help but contrast his situation to Presley's. His own string of failures looked even worse when he was surrounded by signs of Presley's successes. In the past he had enjoyed Presley's company, but now he felt tense and ashamed.[17] These feelings simmered away after he returned home to his dingy trailer, and they ended up having an unusual effect on him; he finally began to develop a sense of drive. As a singer, he had failed, but he was now determined to succeed as a preacher.

Snow's new resolve made him impatient. The prospect of spending four years at a Bible college in order to become ordained did not appeal to him. He wanted to start preaching right away even if it meant postponing his ordination indefinitely. He discovered that he could hold revivals under the auspices of the Assembly of God church so long as he had a preacher's license and renewed it each year. After obtaining his license, he began preaching at tent meetings, youth camps, and crusades throughout the South.[18] At first he used his own life as the basis for most of his sermons, but toward the end of 1959 he added a new sermon to his repertoire—a sermon on the evils of rock 'n' roll.

Snow preached his first anti-rock 'n' roll sermon in Plant City, Florida. The idea to preach on this topic apparently came from a local pastor who knew of Snow's music connections. Throughout his sermon, Snow played up these connections, giving the impression that he was a former rock 'n' roll star whose life had been ruined by performing the music. Like the earlier critics of rock 'n' roll, he focused his sermon on the sexual aspects of the music. "Rock 'n' roll," he said, "primarily appeals to the sensual nature. It produces sexual hysteria in crowds and leads young people to surrender to the passions of the lower nature."[19] He then urged the young people in the audience to free themselves from this "demonic" influence. With the help of the pastor, Snow organized a bonfire and encouraged the teenagers to throw their records into the flames. Some of the teenagers became so caught up in the spirit of the event that they threw in their sheet music, posters, and books along with their records. Presiding over the bonfire was an exhilarating experience for Snow. However, he began to have some misgivings about such burnings after he read accounts of the event in the area newspapers, and he thought that God probably shared these misgivings. According to Snow, God told him, "You don't need this kind of publicity."[20]

Although Snow never sanctioned another public burning, he continued to generate publicity. On 18 February 1960, he began a three-week revival in Savannah, Georgia, during which he vehemently denounced rock 'n' roll. Stories about the revival appeared in several Southern newspapers, including the *Tennessean*, a leading paper from Snow's hometown of Nashville. The *Tennessean* article consisted largely of quotations from Snow's sermon. As the following excerpts demonstrate, his sermon was nearly as racy as the songs he denounced:

> I've studied on it and I've looked around and there's no doubt what rock 'n' roll does—it builds up the sex appetite.
>
> The kids tear their clothes and yell and scream. It excites them and gets them into a frenzy.
>
> Everywhere I go girls come up to me to be saved and they confess improper conduct. And it always happened right after they've been dancing to rock 'n' roll.
>
> Girls as young as nine and ten go to teen towns across the country. And they smoke there and curse and dance to rock 'n' roll, and do all kinds of things and their parents don't know a thing about it.[21]

Snow's revival in Savannah took place shortly before Presley came home from his stint in the army. There was, therefore, a tremendous demand for news stories that in any way related to Presley, and like most news operations, CBS planned to run a story about Presley's return. In the process of conducting their research, the editors at CBS came across an article about Snow's campaign against rock 'n' roll. Since the article played up Snow's connections with Presley, the editors decided to include some information on Snow in their story. They sent a film crew to Savannah where Snow was still preaching and filmed his sermon.

That weekend a four-minute story, most of which dealt with Snow, ran on the network's evening newscast. As a result of this national coverage, he suddenly came to be known as the foremost foe of rock 'n' roll.[22]

Snow fully capitalized on his newfound fame. For the next several years, he crisscrossed the nation, preaching his rock 'n' roll sermon at countless revival meetings. Although his sermon remained basically the same, he made some minor changes to it over the years. The more he preached on the evils of rock 'n' roll, the more he exaggerated the amount of experience he had as a rock 'n' roll singer. His listeners often came away with the impression that he had been in the same league as Presley, Bill Haley, and the other early superstars of rock 'n' roll, which certainly was not the case. He also began adding to his list of problems attributed to rock music. By 1963 the list included fornication, smoking, drinking, drugs, juvenile delinquency, and suicide.[23] It was not until 1965 that Snow finally lost interest in his campaign. Tiring of his transient lifestyle, he decided to take up residence in Nashville and establish a new church, known as the Evangel Temple, on the outskirts of the city. Since that time, Snow has made the church the focus of his life.[24]

When Snow wrote his autobiography in the mid-1970s, he devoted only a few pages to the years he spent preaching against rock 'n' roll. He did not apologize for his campaign, but he made it clear that he no longer viewed rock 'n' roll as the primary scourge of modern times. In fact, the musical combo that performed in his church included a lead guitar, a rhythm guitar, a bass and a full drum set—the same instruments found in traditional rock bands.[25] Snow's change of heart makes one skeptical about the motivations for his earlier denunciations of rock 'n' roll. His campaign was likely fueled by factors that had little to do with the music he condemned. He seems to have had difficulties dealing with Presley's success, and this may well be why he harbored bitter feelings toward rock 'n' roll. The evidence also suggests that he used rock 'n' roll as an excuse for the problems that he had as a young man. All of the problems that he associated with rock 'n' roll were problems that he himself experienced. Of course, these problems had much more to do with his tense relationship with his father and his unstable childhood than with his dabblings in rock music, but the music served as a convenient scapegoat. Finally, there was probably an element of opportunism in his campaign. Like most performers, he tried to please his audience, and his audience responded enthusiastically to his sermon on rock 'n' roll. So long as they did, he felt no pressure to prepare other sermons.

Snow's motives may have been questionable, but there can be little doubt that he managed to tap a vein of genuine reaction. The people who flocked to his sermons felt at odds with the changing nature of American culture. They attended revival meetings not only because they wanted to revive their religious faith, but also because they wanted to revive the values and beliefs of an earlier time. For these people, Snow's attacks on rock 'n' roll took on a symbolic quality. Although they probably knew very little about rock music, that did not stop them from identifying with Snow's sermon, for in their minds rock 'n' roll represented modern decadence. More than anything else, these people objected to the growing acceptance of sexuality, especially the sexualtiy of young people. They still clung to the idea of childhood innocence, and Snow usually worked this idea into his sermons. By arguing that rock 'n' roll caused teenagers to become interested in sex rather than reflecting a pre-existing interest, Snow told his audience exactly what they wanted to hear, thus assuring them of the continuing validity of their long-held ideas.

8.

The New Right Versus
the New Realists

After giving up his campaign against rock 'n' roll, Jimmy Snow
went for over ten years without attracting much attention outside
of Nashville. In October 1976, however, he again made national
news. This time he appeared in a *Newsweek* cover story entitled
"Born Again: The Year of the Evangelicals." The article included
biographies of Snow and five other "born again" Christians, but
it focused on the growing political power of evangelicals. Prior to
the 1970s, according to the article, the political clout of evangelicals had been undercut by geographical and denominational
differences, but these differences were beginning to break down,
in part because of the emergence of several prominent television
evangelists. Through the skillful use of nationally syndicated
television programs, these men attracted large numbers of followers from various regions and denominations. They accomplished
this feat by emphasizing the conservative religious, moral, and
political beliefs held in common by most evangelicals despite
their occasional doctrinal disputes.[1]

Within a few years of the publication of the *Newsweek*
article, the political power of evangelicals and other conservative
Christians became even greater. Dubbed the "New Right" by the
news media, these conservative activists launched a multi-
pronged assault on various aspects of American society that they

deemed immoral, including abortions, the Equal Rights Amendment, and pornography. Also on their long list of targets were
some of the most popular children's books of the 1970s. They
especially disliked Judy Blume's and Norma Klein's bestselling
novels. Pointing to the books' candid treatment of sexual matters,
they argued that these books encourage sexual promiscuity
among young people and should therefore be censored.

The critics of Blume and Klein believed that sexuality has no
place in children's literature. For a long time, this view was
shared by most authors and publishers of children's books. While
other aspects of American society began acknowledging the
sexuality of children and adolescents as early as the 1940s,
mainstream children's literature remained wedded to the notion
of childhood innocence. Even during the sexual revolution of the
1960s, children's authors hardly ever dealt with sexuality in their
books. In the early 1970s, however, a number of children's
authors began questioning many of the taboos that earlier authors
had strictly observed.[2] These new authors felt that children's
literature should reflect reality the way it really is, which is why
they became known as the "New Realists." Of these authors,
Judy Blume and Norma Klein took the lead in breaking the taboo
against writing about sex.

Neither Blume nor Klein originally intended to revolutionize
children's literature. In fact, both were largely unaware that they
were breaking taboos when they began including references to
sexuality in their children's books. This seeming ignorance of
these taboos can be attributed to several factors. To begin with,
their childhoods differed considerably from the childhoods of
most Americans. Both authors were born in 1938 to affluent,
liberal, and well-educated parents who took a fairly permissive
approach to child-rearing. Also, both spent much of their childhoods in the New York City area where they were exposed to a
wide variety of cultural influences. As a result of their childhood
experiences, they grew up being a bit more sophisticated than
many of their contemporaries. Upon entering adulthood in the
1960s, they became enmeshed in the social and political events of
that tumultuous decade, and this distanced them even further
from the more conservative elements of American society.[3] Finally, in Klein's view, their religious orientation predisposed
them to disregard taboos:

I think it's significant that Judy Blume and I, two of the children's authors most frequently attacked for our openness, are both Jewish. American Jewish authors have often been more irreverent and iconoclastic—Erica Jong and Philip Roth are just two examples out of many.[4]

The circumstances surrounding each author's entrance into the children's book world allowed them to write their first children's books without having to concern themselves much about breaking taboos. Shortly after Blume became a children's author, she came into contact with Richard Jackson and Robert Verrone, the founders of the new publishing firm called Bradbury Press. Unlike the great majority of children's book publishers, Jackson and Verrone felt that children's literature was too encumbered with taboos. Consequently, they actually encouraged Blume and the other authors they published to write freely about sex and other controversial topics.[5] When Klein wrote her first book for children, she knew little about the dynamics of children's book publishing, having spent ten years writing short stories for adults. Thus, though she violated several taboos in her book, she did so unwittingly. She also had the good fortune of sending her manuscript to Fabio Coen, one of the few established editors of children's books who was willing to accept potentially controversial books.[6] In other words, Blume and Klein felt somewhat freer to experiment than most children's authors writing during the same time period.

Although both Blume and Klein became well-known children's authors in the early 1970s, Blume entered the field slightly before Klein. Blume's first children's book, *The One in the Middle Is the Green Kangaroo*, came out in 1969 and was followed by *Iggie's House* in 1970. While these two books broke no new ground, her third book, *Are You There God? It's Me, Margaret* (1970), made history for being the first children's book to deal frankly with a girl's anxieties about menstruation and breast development. Over the course of the decade, Blume published nine more books, several of which include sexually related material. *Then Again, Maybe I Won't* (1971) refers to wet dreams, and *Deenie* (1973) contains a few passages on masturbation. In 1975 she published *Forever*, a young adult novel that focuses on a teenage love affair during which the couple eventually engages in sexual intercourse. These novels, along with Blume's other books, attracted tremendous followings, making Blume the best-selling children's author of the 1970s and '80s.

Klein published her first children's book, *Mom, the Wolf Man, and Me*, in 1972. The story revolves around the relationship between an eleven-year-old girl and her single mother. What makes the story unusual is that the mother has never been married, and she has a male friend who occasionally spends the night with her. Klein went on to publish sixteen more books for young readers before the end of the decade. The issue of sexuality figures in many of these, including *Naomi in the Middle* (1974) and *It's OK If You Don't Love Me* (1977). *Naomi in the Middle* focuses on a seven-year-old girl who is trying to adjust to the impending birth of a sibling. Responding to the girl's questions, the mother in the story explains how conception occurs. In *It's OK If You Don't Love Me*, a novel for young adults, Klein chronicles the love affair of a teenage couple. Like Blume's *Forever*, the book includes several sexually explicit passages. Also like *Forever*, it achieved bestseller status.

For much of the 1970s, Blume's and Klein's books aroused little controversy, and what controversy there was seemed insignificant even to Blume and Klein. The first time one of Blume's books was banned from a library, she dismissed it as an isolated case. The incident occurred shortly after the publication of *Are You There God? It's Me, Margaret*. As she had done with her earlier books, she donated a copy to her children's elementary school, but the principal disapproved of the book and refused to allow it in the school library. In recalling this event, Blume said, "I just thought he was a nut. It never occurred to me that it was going to happen again."[7] And for the next half dozen years it did not. During this same period, only one of Klein's children's books ran into a censorship problem, and it was not very serious. In 1973 a mother in Anchorage, Alaska, attempted to have *Mom, the Wolf Man, and Me* banned from the city's elementary schools because she claimed it was not "true to life." However, by a vote of five to one, the school board refused to remove the book.[8] Thus, neither Blume nor Klein has any reason to suspect that her books were about to come under intense censorship pressures.

The major attacks on Blume and Klein began in the late 1970s. This development was reflected in the pages of the *News-*

letter on Intellectual Freedom, an American Library Association publication that closely monitors censorship activity. Throughout 1976 none of Blume's or Klein's books appeared in its reports, but in 1977 each author had a book that was listed as a target of censors. The first case took place in Rockville, Maryland, where both *Naomi in the Middle* and *Forever* were removed from library shelves on the grounds that they were "unnecessarily explicit" and dealt with "adult topics."[9] *Naomi in the Middle* was also involved in a case in Brockport, New York. Although the Brockport school board denied a request that the book be banned from the elementary school library, the book's availability was restricted to children whose parents gave them written permission to read it.[10] In 1978 and '79, several more cases were reported, some of which involved additional titles. In Gate City, Tennessee, *It's OK If You Don't Love Me* came under attack by a citizens' group that called the book "pornographic,"[11] while in Richmond, Virginia, an irate mother led a successful effort to restrict the availability of *Deenie* and *Then Again, Maybe I Won't.*[12]

In the early 1980s, the controversy surrounding Blume and Klein greatly intensified. According to the *Newsletter on Intellectual Freedom*, there were seven censorship cases involving their books in 1980, increasing to fourteen the following year. This sudden increase was related to the emergence of several conservative organizations, such as Rev. Jerry Falwell's Moral Majority, Phyllis Schlafly's Eagle Forum, Mel and Norma Gabler's Educational Research Analysts, and Beverly LaHaye's Concerned Women for America. Some of the leaders of these organizations urged their followers to take action against certain books. For example, Rev. H. Lamarr Mooneyham, the chair of the North Carolina chapter of the Moral Majority, compiled a list of twelve books that he and his followers considered immoral. Although Mooneyham focused on textbooks, he included *Forever* on his list. In April 1981, he mailed the list to eight thousand North Carolinians and asked them to file complaints against these books. "The success of this thing," he said, "is going to rest completely upon the concern of parents. It's up to them to initiate the confrontation with the people on their particular school boards."[13] This encouragement led many people to initiate censorship attempts.

In addition to being lambasted in the house organs of several conservative groups, Blume and Klein were criticized in a number of national publications,[14] which generated other censorship cases. One of the most damaging articles appeared in an April 1980 issue of the *National Enquirer*, a popular tabloid sold in supermarkets. Entitled "Why You'd Better Look at Your Children's Books," the article makes *Are You There God? It's Me, Margaret* and other books by Blume and Klein sound as lurid as possible. After reading the article, a number of parents became upset. In Montello, Wisconsin, the article led to the formation of a parents' group called Concerned Citizens. As its first project, the group attempted to have Blume's books removed from the public school libraries. When this effort failed, they checked out the books and refused to return them on the due date. In lieu of the missing books, they scattered religious tracts throughout the library.[15]

As the 1980s progressed, the assaults on Blume and Klein continued unabated. Other children's authors also came under attack, including Robert Cormier, Paul Zindel, Betty Miles, Maurice Sendak, and Harry Mazer. Once it became clear that this was not a passing fad, the opponents of censorhip became very concerned. People for the American Way, the National Coalition Against Censorship, and other civil liberties groups began collecting and disseminating data on censorship cases in an effort to make the public aware of the magnitude of the problem. One of the most revealing of these reports was released by the American Booksellers Association in September 1982. Rather than focus entirely on recent censorship cases, the association looked to the past. It compiled a list of the most frequently banned books since the advent of book publishing. As the following summary shows, Blume and Klein figure prominently on the list:

> Alexander Solzhenitsyn and Judy Blume tie as authors with the greatest number of titles banned: eight. D. H. Lawrence, Ernest Hemingway, Richard Brautigan and William Faulkner each have six; Norma Klein and Kurt Vonnegut, five; and Daniel Defoe and Theodore Dreiser, four.[16]

From 1982 through 1985, the *Newsletter for Intellectual Freedom* covered nearly sixty attempts to ban books by Blume and Klein. Although these attempts were scattered around the country, almost all of them were initiated by the New Right. Of all these attempts, the one that attracted the most attention took place in Peoria, Illinois, in November 1984. Unlike most censorship cases, the situation in Peoria did not begin with the filing of a formal complaint. Instead, Earl Robertson, the director of libraries for the Peoria school district, along with Dennis Gainey, the district's associate superintendent, took it upon themselves to remove three of Blume's books from the elementary school libraries even though no one had expressed any objections to the books. Two of the books, *Then Again, Maybe I Won't* and *Deenie*, were banned because of their "sexual content," while *Blubber*, a story about the persecution of an overweight girl at the hands of her classmates, was censored for its "strong language." Gainey justified this action on the grounds that it was "the prudent thing to do."[17]

The unilateral nature of this decision offended many people, including some residents of Peoria. The president of the local chapter of the American Civil Liberties Union and several vocal parents asked that the books be returned. Their calls were soon joined by a chorus of other voices from around the nation. Immediately after the decision was announced, Blume, her publisher, and a spokesperson for the American Library Association all issued statements denouncing it.[18] Soon thereafter, the Peoria school board began receiving protest letters, one of which was signed by eight of the nation's most respected children's authors, including Natalie Babbitt, Madeleine L'Engle, and Katherine Paterson. These authors called the decision an act of "intolerance" and criticized the argument that the books should be made available only to older children because it "reduces the level of library reading fare for all students to a level that the board deems acceptable for the youngest students."[19] The case also generated a tremendous amount of publicity. The Associated Press, several television news programs, the *New York Times*, and many other news operations covered the story. Faced with all this pressure and publicity, the school board voted to overrule the decision of the administrators and return the books to the library shelves.[20]

As the Peoria case clearly demonstrates, the attempts to censor Blume's and Klein's books have not gone unopposed. In almost every case, the books have attracted at least as many supporters as detractors, and more often than not supporters have succeeded in keeping the contested books on the shelves. The detractors have also failed to curtail the popularity of these books. Despite all the hullabaloo, most of Blume's and Klein's books have continued to sell very well. It would be a mistake, in other words, to interpret the surge of censorship attempts as a sign that the New Realists have fallen out of favor with the entire adult population. On the whole, the evidence suggests that most Americans have not embraced the New Right's position that children should be sheltered from all references to sexuality.

What the surge of censorship attempts does show is that many of the New Right disapprove of the growing toleration of childhood sexuality. In part, their disapproval stems from the traditional Christian doctrine that all forms of premarital sex are sinful. It also, however, reflects their belief that an interest in sexuality is not an intrinsic part of children's psychological makeup. They believe instead that children who show an interest in this area must have absorbed it from outside influences, such as Blume's or Klein's books. Thus, in their minds, allowing children to read such books runs the risk of introducing previously unknown forms of sinful behavior into the lives of innocent children. This concern can be seen in the statements they make about the books. A Baptist minister in Florida, for example, said that the reason he wanted to censor *Deenie* was because "it described the act of masturbation and that amounts to a how-to manual."[21] In other words, their attempts to ban Blume's and Klein's books are part of an effort to perpetuate children's ignorance of sexual matters, for as they see it, ignorance and innocence are one and the same. As far as sexuality is concerned, they clearly believe that the thought is as bad as the deed. They, of course, are not the first to equate ignorance with childhood innocence. This idea runs through nearly every controversy in the history of American children's culture. The New Right has simply tied this idea directly to the issue of sexuality.

9.

The Tennessee Textbook Controversy

Throughout the first half of the 1980s, the attacks on Judy Blume and Norma Klein came fast and furious, but they were not especially effective or well organized. In most cases, a parent or a small group of parents attempted, usually without success, to force their local school board into removing particular titles from the school libraries. These parents generally lost interest in their campaigns once they were given an opportunity to voice their complaints. Although these parents derived a certain amount of moral support from various New Right organizations, they seldom received direct orders or financial assistance from these groups. The national leadership of the New Right clearly disapproved of Blume's and Klein's books, but they were more concerned about textbooks.

At first glance, the New Right's attacks on Blume's and Klein's novels appear to have little in common with their attacks on textbooks. In the case of the novels, their criticisms focus mostly on sexuality, whereas in the case of the textbooks, their objections have more to do with religion. There is, however, a common thread that runs through both cases, and that is the desire to preserve the ignorance of children. Just as they object to Blume's *Deenie* on the grounds that it might teach children about masturbation, they object to some textbooks because the books might teach children about diverse value systems and religious beliefs. Needless to say, the New Right's desire to keep children in ignorance of the broader world has led to some serious confrontations with "professional" educators. Several of these confrontations have ended up in the courts, including a highly publicized case that originated in the mountains of eastern Tennessee. Since this is not far from the site of the famous Scopes trial, the case came to be known as "Scopes II."

From the beginning of its ascendancy in the mid-1970s, the New Right frequently attacked textbooks. Initially, these attacks were led by Mel and Norma Gabler, a Texas couple who specialized in identifying "objectionable" material in textbooks. They felt that textbooks should reinforce the beliefs of conservative Christians, and if the books failed in this regard, the Gablers would denounce them in their newsletter.[1] The Gablers were soon joined by a host of other religious conservatives who disapproved of certain textbooks. Foremost among these were the Rev. Tim and Beverly LaHaye from San Diego, California. Tim LaHaye sharply criticized textbooks in *The Battle for the Public Schools*, one of a series of New Right manifestoes he wrote in the early 1980s. While her husband was writing these tracts, Beverly LaHaye founded a conservative women's group known as Concerned Women for America (CWA). It quickly grew into one of the most powerful organizations of the New Right. As its president, Beverly LaHaye tirelessly campaigned against such things as the Equal Rights Amendment, abortion, sex education, and (not surprisingly) "immoral" textbooks.[2]

Not content with simply issuing position statements, LaHaye and the other leaders of her organization decided to take a more activist approach. To this end, they raised a considerable war chest. They also hired attorney Michael Farris, the former executive director of the Washington state chapter of the Moral Majority, to serve as their legal counsel. With Farris's help, LaHaye hoped to take her campaign against textbooks to the courts. She and Farris especially wanted to become involved in a case that had the potential of establishing a legal pretext for banning textbooks. They therefore carefully evaluated all the reports they heard about disputes over textbooks in the hopes of finding one that would serve as an ideal test case. In November 1983, they learned of a conflict over textbooks in Church Hill, Tennessee, and from what they heard they had a hunch they had found their case.

The Church Hill case can be traced back to the beginning of the 1983–84 school year. Like all the other elementary and middle schools in Hawkins County, the schools in Church Hill were using a new series of textbooks in their reading classes. Published by Holt, Rinehart & Winston, the series was designed to be used in grades one through eight. A committee of reading teachers from Hawkins County had selected the Holt series from a list of state-approved textbooks because they were impressed with the literary quality of stories that appeared in the series.[3] Not everyone, however, agreed with their assessment. The schools had not been open for more than a week when William Snodgrass, the Hawkins County school superintendent, received a complaint about the opening story in *Riders on the Earth*, the reader used in the sixth grade.

The complaint came from Vicki Rogers, a conservative fundamentalist and mother of four school-aged children. It was certainly not the first time that she had complained to a school official. Just the previous school year, she had objected to a field trip that her sixth-grade son was scheduled to attend because it involved viewing a PG movie and eating at a restaurant that served beer. That same year she had also complained when she discovered that her daughter had heard rock music at school. Her new complaint, however, concerned a story entitled "A Visit to Mars." The story is actually an excerpt from *The Angry Planet*, a 1946 science-fiction novel by John Kier Cross. Frost read the story in order to help her daughter, Rebecca, answer the reading questions. The story deals with telepathy, to which Frost objected on religious grounds. She expressed her concern to Snodgrass, but he refused to take her complaint seriously and made a joke about cutting the story out with a pair of scissors.[4]

Snodgrass's response left Frost feeling frustrated and angry. Rather than drop her complaint, as Snodgrass had hoped she would, she decided to launch a campaign against the entire reader. Immediately after calling Snodgrass, she began reading the rest of the stories in *Riders on the Earth* and found that she had religious objections to practically all of them. Many of the stories mention myths or non-Western religions, and she felt that these stories taught "false religion." Other stories include references to magic, and Frost saw this as being anti-Biblical. Still others portray girls in nonpassive roles, and this, according to

Frost, violates the roles that God set forth for the sexes.[5] She discussed her objections with her husband, Roger Frost, and her best friend, Jennie Wilson, and together they decided to denounce the book at a public meeting. They obtained permission from James Salley, the principal of the Church Hill Middle School, to hold the meeting at the school and publicized the event through radio and newspaper announcements. The meeting took place on 1 September 1983, and was attended by over one hundred people. The two chief speakers were Vicki Frost, who spelled out her objections to the book, and the Rev. Billy Christian, a local minister who spoke out against telepathy.[6]

Not long after this initial meeting, the conflict over the Holt series greatly intensified. The issue was brought up at the Hawkins County School board meeting on 8 September at which time the board reaffirmed its commitment to keeping the series on the list of required textbooks. In response to the board's action, Frost redoubled her efforts. Rather than limit her attacks to *Riders on the Earth*, she began criticizing the entire series. She contacted the Gablers in Texas and asked them to send her their report on the series. She also began soliciting the support of other parents who shared her religious beliefs. On 22 September about thirteen of Frost's supporters met and formed a short-lived organization called Citizens Organized for Better Schools (COBS). Although the group elected Robert Mozert, a local insurance adjuster, as its director, Frost was clearly the driving force behind the group. Initially, the group had a long list of objectives, including implementing a strict dress code for students, requiring the daily recitation of the Pledge of Allegiance, and mandating a moment of silence at the beginning of each school day. Soon, however, the group decided to focus its efforts on the Holt series.[7]

Frost, Mozert, and some of the other members of COBS spent much of October and November in a prolonged confrontation with the school board. Several of them attended the board meeting on 13 October and demanded, among other things, that their children not be required to read any of the books in the Holt series. About a week later they called a public meeting during which they attacked both the board and the Holt series for supporting "secular humanism." They also began distributing a pamphlet published by the Gablers entitled *Humanism in Text-*

books. Most importantly, a few of them ordered their children not to read the Holt textbooks. This action placed the teachers and principals from the affected schools in a difficult situation. At first, some attempts were made to accommodate these children by providing them with alternative textbooks and dismissing them from class whenever material from the Holt series was being discussed. It soon became apparent, though, that this arrangement was untenable. It not only deprived these students of actual reading instruction, but it also seriously disrupted class discussions and other learning activities. In light of these problems, the school board passed a resolution on 10 November which prohibited the use of alternative textbooks in reading classes.[8]

The passage of this resolution set the stage for a showdown between COBS and the school board. Frost, Mozert and a few other parents forbade their children to attend the mandatory reading lessons so long as the Holt readers were being used. Several school officials warned the parents that this action violated school rules, but the parents persisted. On 15 November the principal of the Church Hill Middle School responded to this open act of defiance by temporarily suspending the ten students who were not attending class.[9] A week later the scene of the showdown moved to the Church Hill Elementary School where Frost's daughter, Sarah, attended second grade. On 22 November Frost came to the school in order to remove her daughter from class during the reading lesson, but was ordered off the school grounds by Jean Price, the principal. The next day Frost again came to take her daughter out of class; however, this time Price had her arrested for trespassing.[10]

Several of Frost's friends became very concerned when they learned of her encounters with Price. They felt that Frost needed legal assistance, but they were not sure where to turn for help. One of them, however, was a member of Concerned Women for America, and she suggested that Frost call the organization and ask for advice. At the time, Frost was only vaguely aware of CWA, but she made the call and was connected with Michael Farris. He knew nothing about the case, but once he heard her account of it, he immediately decided to throw his and the organizations's support behind Frost and the other parents whose children had been suspended. After substantiating Frost's story and consulting with the leadership of CWA, he agreed to take on the case free of charge.[11]

The reason Farris wanted to become involved with the case was he felt that if it could be kept alive, it had the potential of generating a tremendous amount of publicity. Up until this time, only the local media had covered the story, but Farris was sure this situation would change once the leaders of the New Right heard about the students' suspensions and Frost's arrest. Farris knew these could easily be portrayed as examples of Christians being persecuted by secular humanists, and this was exactly the type of story that the television evangelists and other New Right spokespersons loved to publicize. Farris wanted to encourage the publicity because of its possible political ramifications. As he later stated in an interview, such publicity tends to "foster political activity by Christians, and the result will be increased pressure on the public schools."[12]

Farris also believed he had a good chance of getting the case heard in federal court. In order to do this, he had to show that the plaintiffs' constitutional rights had been violated, and Farris thought he could make such an argument. He intended to base his argument on the free exercise clause of the First Amendment. This clause guarantees the right to exercise one's religion without governmental interference. As Farris saw it, requiring students to read stories that offended their parents' religious beliefs could be interpreted as a violation of their and their parents' right to exercise their religion. He knew that if the court agreed to hear his argument, it would be a landmark case.

In late November, Farris traveled to Church Hill where he met with Frost, Mozert, and several other potential plaintiffs. He told them that before he could file a lawsuit he needed them to articulate more clearly the ways in which the Holt textbooks offended their religious beliefs. Several lengthy meetings quickly ensued during which they listed their specific religious objections to each of the seventeen books in the series.[13] They came up with well over two hundred objections. These included an objection to *Rumpelstiltskin* because it is not "accompanied by an explanation of the evil of magic,"[14] an objection to *The Wizard of Oz* because "it portrays witches as good,"[15] and an objection to *The Diary of Anne Frank* because it "supports different roads to one God."[16]

At the same time that these meetings were taking place, Farris contacted all the families who had children suspended in an attempt to sign them on as plaintiffs. He succeeded in attracting a total of thirty-nine plaintiffs from eleven families. Of these, twenty-one were adults and eighteen were children. On 2 December 1983, Farris filed a lawsuit in the United States District Court on behalf of these plaintiffs. He named as defendants the Hawkins County Public Schools, the five school board members, the superintendent, and four principals. As it was originally worded, the suit asked that the suspended students be reinstated, that the students not be compelled to read the Holt textbooks, and that damages be paid to the plaintiffs.[17]

A certain amount of showmanship attended the filing of the lawsuit. Immediately after he filed the necessary papers at the federal courthouse in Greeneville, Tennessee, Farris held an emotional press conference. While still standing on the courthouse steps, he proclaimed, "This is the first time an evangelical, fundamentalist group has been forced to court by the negative actions of a school district."[18] That evening, Concerned Women for America sponsored a public rally in Kingsport, a town near Church Hill, during which the plaintiffs were treated as martyred heroes.[19]

While many on the New Right viewed the plaintiffs as heroes, most of the local residents did not. These people thought of themselves as conservatives, yet they were not convinced that the Holt textbooks posed a serious threat to their children. Many of them actually came to the support of the school board. In early December, a group of parents formed an organization called Citizens Advocating the Right to Education (CARE), which was designed to counter the influence of COBS. CARE asked area residents to show their support of the school board by attending a mass meeting, and approximately one thousand people came, far more than ever attended a COBS meeting. A group of students also came to the defense of the school board. Calling themselves Students Against COBS, the students complained that COBS was needlessly tarnishing the reputation of the school system. A local ministerial association lent its support to the school board as well, saying that it had investigated the charges against the textbooks and was unable to identify any significant problems. It was the general consensus that if the plaintiffs disliked the public school curriculum, they should simply send their children to private schools.[20] Most of the plaintiffs soon came to the same decision, but this did not stop them from pursuing their lawsuit.

The lawsuit practically died shortly after it was filed. On 15 March 1984, United States District Court Judge Thomas G. Hull ruled that a trial was not necessary because the plaintiffs did not demonstrate that their constitutional rights had been violated. "The First Amendment," he wrote, "does not protect the plaintiffs from exposure to morally offensive value systems or from exposure to antithetical religious ideas."[21] Farris, of course, disagreed and appealed to the United States Court of Appeals for the Sixth Circuit. In June 1985, this court reversed Hull's ruling, citing procedural problems. Thus, the case was sent back to district court, and preparations for a trial commenced.[22]

Some major developments took place before the case ever came to trial. On 17 January 1986, four of the eleven families who had originally filed suit withdrew from the case, leaving fourteen adults and fourteen children listed as plaintiffs. While Farris stayed on as the plaintiffs' lead counsel, he was joined by two of CWA's other attorneys. Most of the plaintiffs' legal costs continued to be absorbed by CWA, but several other New Right organizations provided some financial assistance. The defendants also benefited from outside help. People for the American Way, an organization devoted to protecting civil liberties, began providing financial assistance to the defendants. This assistance enabled them to retain Timothy Dyk, a prominent lawyer from Washington, D.C., to serve as their lead counsel.[23]

In July 1986, Judge Hull finally began the trial. Since it was a bench trial, no jury was involved. Over the course of the trial, Farris developed his argument that the Hawkins County School Board was violating the plaintiffs' free exercise rights by requiring the students to read books that offended their religious beliefs. He concluded by requesting that the schools provide alternative readers. Dyk did not question the sincerity of the plaintiffs' religious beliefs or their contention that the Holt textbooks offended these beliefs. Rather, he argued that the plaintiffs could easily avoid exposing their children to the material that they found offensive by either sending their children to private school or educating them at home. They were not being compelled, in other words, to perform acts that conflicted with their free exercise rights. Dyk further argued that the state and county have a compelling interest in teaching critical reading skills to those children who attend the public schools and that the schools cannot teach these skills without making use of required readings. This compelling governmental interest, he concluded, should override whatever objections that parents might have to the readings.[24]

The testimony lasted for eight days, ending on 23 July 1986. In addition to hearing the participants in the case tell their stories, Hull heard the testimony of several expert witnesses. The most prominent of the plaintiffs' expert witnesses was Mel Gabler, who argued that the Holt textbooks discriminated against fundamentalists.[25] The defendants' star witness was Robert Coles, a child psychiatrist who teaches at Harvard University. Coles focused his testimony on the harmful psychological ramifications of segregating children on the basis of their religious beliefs.[26] After the testimony, the counsel for both sides filed written briefs, and in September they presented their final oral arguments before Hull.

On 24 October 1986, Hull released his decision, finding for the plaintiffs. "The defendants," he wrote, "burdened the plaintiffs' right of free exercise of religion" by requiring "the plaintiff-students to read from the Holt series." While he denied the plaintiffs' request that the schools provide the plaintiff-students with alternative readers, he ruled that the students were "entitled to opt out of the Hawkins County Public School reading program while still enjoying the benefit of the rest of the curriculum." As he envisioned it, the students would "withdraw to a study hall or to the library" during the regular reading periods, and after school they "would study reading with a parent." He also ruled that the plaintiffs were entitled to damages, but he did not specify how much.[27] In December, he conducted a hearing on damages after which he awarded the plaintiffs $51,531 to cover the costs involved with sending their children to private Christian schools.[28]

Predictably, Michael Farris and Beverly LaHaye reacted jubilantly to Hull's decision. Speaking at a press conference in Washington, D.C., Farris proclaimed, "Those who wanted to throw children out of school because of their religion have been decisively defeated."[29] LaHaye echoed Farris's sentiments. "Today's decision," she said, "is a tremendous step forward for religious freedom in America."[30] Many others, however, feared that the decision could interfere with the running of the public schools. Anthony Podesta, then president of People for the American Way, called the ruling "a recipe for disaster for public education," and that it invited "every sect in the country to pick and choose which parts of the curriculum it will accept."[31] Joan Beck, a syndicated columnist, was especially worried about the impact of the decision on textbooks. She predicted that "publishers will be tripping all over each other to assure school boards that nothing in their texts could make the schools vulnerable to a lawsuit." This would result, she argued, in reducing "the content of textbooks to mind numbing mush."[32]

Immediately after Hull released his decision, the attorneys for the school board announced plans to fight it. As Dyk told a group of reporters, "This is not the end of the road. We intend to take this case as far as is necessary to get this decision reversed."[33] The school board appealed the case to the United States Court of Appeals for the Sixth District. In the "Brief of Appellants," Dyk reiterated many of the arguments he had originally made before Hull. He also criticized the "opt-out" remedy that Hull had ordered. Dyk pointed out that the Hawkins County schools use an integrated curriculum, which means that discussions of reading material take place during the entire school day, not just during a set period. Thus, in order to comply with Hull's order, teachers "would either have to avoid or discourage the discussion of 'objectionable' themes and ideas or put them on hold while the plaintiff-students were excused from the classroom." This, he maintained, would significantly disrupt the class. He also argued that the opt-out remedy would lead to religious divisiveness, lead other parents to make similar demands for exemption, and discourage schools from including important but controversial material in their curricula.[34]

On 24 August 1987, the court of appeals overruled Hull's decision. All the members of the three judge panel agreed that the plaintiffs' constitutional rights had not been violated. As Chief Judge Pierce Lively explained in his opinion, requiring the plaintiff-students to read the Holt textbooks is not tantamount to requiring them to believe everything that the books contain:

The requirement that public school students study a basal reader series chosen by the school authorities does not create an unconstitutional burden under the Free Exercise Clause when the students are not required to affirm or deny a belief or engage or refrain from engaging in a practice prohibited or required by their religion. There was no evidence that the conduct required of the students was forbidden by their religion. Rather, the witnesses testified that reading the Holt series "could" or "might" lead the students to come to conclusions that were contrary to teachings of their religious beliefs. This is not sufficient to establish an unconstitutional burden.

The judgment of the District Court granting injunctive relief and damages is reversed, and the case is remanded with directions to dismiss the complaint.[35]

Farris appealed this ruling to the Supreme Court, but the Court refused to hear the case. Thus, the ruling of the court of appeals remained standing, ending a legal battle that lasted a full four years. There can be little doubt that the case would never have lasted for so long or have taken on such importance if it were not for two factors: the fierce determination of Vicki Frost and Robert Mozert and the backing of CWA. Each year hundreds of parents file complaints against textboks, but most of these parents quiet down after they have made their objections known. Certainly very few of them feel so strongly about their objections that they would engage in an act of civil disobedience, which is essentially what Frost did. The determination of Frost and Mozert, however, was not enough to push this case into the national spotlight. Without CWA's money and legal assistance, Frost and Mozert would have had little chance of bringing their case to court let alone engaging in a lengthy legal battle. Thus, even though the plaintiffs appear to have lost their case, the simple fact that it remained in litigation for so many years demonstrated the growing clout of CWA and, by extension, the New Right.

In the process of waging their legal battle against the Holt textbooks, the plaintiffs and those who supported them made a statement about their attitudes toward education. For these people, the withholding of information is as an important part of education as imparting values and knowledge. There are many aspects of contemporary society that these people find objectionable, and they would rather that their children be kept in ignorance of these things. They remain unconvinced by the argument that children need to learn about the complexities of the modern world in order to cope with life, for in their opinion the only righteous way to cope with much of the modern world is to reject it. They correctly assume that it is easier to reject that which is alien and unexplained than that which is familiar and understood.

10.

The Idealization of
the Pretelevision Child

Much of the literature that the New Right puts out is steeped in nostalgia. The writers of this literature often set up a simple dichotomy between the past and the present. They argue that in the past all was right with the world, but somehow everything has gone awry in recent years. When writing about education, for example, they imply that the public schools used to be run in accordance with Christianity, but now the schools have been taken over by a group of secular humanists who are out to destroy the Christian way of life. This tendency to idealize the past can also be seen in their attitudes toward children. They describe the children of yesteryear as innocent, happy, and well behaved, while the children of today are described as jaded, sullen, and disrespectful.

The idea that contemporary children are somehow less innocent then children from earlier generations is not limited to the New Right. Since the late 1970s, several media critics, including Marie Winn, David Elkind, and Neil Postman, have made the same argument. Although they do not share the political and religious views of the New Right, they agree with the New Right's condemnation of contemporary child-rearing practices and beliefs. In the opinion of these critics, today's children are being robbed of a happy and innocent childhood. They, however, do not blame the dissolution of childhood innocence on secular humanism, permissiveness, or any of the other bugaboos of the New Right. Instead, television is the chief culprit.

These critics are certainly not the first to express a concern over the effects of television viewing on children. As early as the mid-1950s, some people began complaining that children's television programs were too violent. Over the years, this concern gradually increased until it came to a head in 1968. The assassinations and riots of that year sent many people looking for the causes of violent behavior, and some singled out children's television programs. A number of these people formed a group known as Action for Children's Television (ACT), which focused its attention on changing the content of children's programs. Through a petition to the Federal Communications Commission, ACT attempted to force the networks as well as individual stations to replace violent cartoons with educational programs.[1]

While Winn, Elkind, and Postman share ACT's concern about the content of children's programs, they feel that this is only one aspect of a far broader problem. In their opinions, children are adversely affected by watching television programs even if the programs contain no violence. All three of these critics have published books in which they discuss their theories on this subject. Winn led the way with the publication of *The Plug-In Drug* in 1977. She continued her argument in her next book, *Children Without Childhood* (1983), as well as in two lengthy articles published in the *New York Times Magazine*. Elkind stated his objections to television in *The Hurried Child* (1981), while Postman expressed his views in *The Disappearance of Childhood* (1982). In addition to their anti-television themes, all of these publications contain an idealized image of the pretelevision child.

As its title implies, Marie Winn's *The Plug-In Drug* is based on the idea that children can become addicted to television in much the same way that people can become addicted to heroin and other drugs. In order to support this thesis, she relies on a series of interviews that she conducted with parents and children. Thus, the book is filled with anecdotes about children who became "mesmerized" by television. These young "television zombies," as she refers to them, are described as being in a kind of "stupor," a problem she attributes to the passive nature of television viewing.[2] She then lists a number of negative side effects which she associates with this "addiction." These include the underdevelopment of children's verbal skills, a greater tendency for them to engage in antisocial behavior, a decrease in the amount of time they spend reading and playing, and a deterioration of their relationships with their parents.

Sandwiched between her attacks on television is a short chapter entitled "How Parents Survived Before Television." In this chapter, Winn paints a rosy picture of family life during the 1930s and '40s, the period of her own childhood. A typical mother from this period, according to Winn, observed her child "with an eagle eye" and was always on the lookout for new projects to amuse the youngster. As a result, the mother was closely attuned to her child's development and had a "more satisfying relationship with her child, with greater opportunities for shared pleasures as well as a reduced likelihood of misunderstanding and inadvertently inflicted suffering."[3] Winn argues that fathers were also more involved with child-rearing. She writes that when the typical father came home from work, he often played with his offspring for an hour or so while his wife "went for a walk or took a bath."[4] As for the children, Winn claims that they spent their time contentedly playing, reading, and taking naps.[5]

In her next several publications, Winn more fully explains why she feels childhood has changed since the advent of television. In "What Became of Innocence?," an article published in the *New York Times Magazine* in January 1981, she refers to the pretelevision era as the "Golden Age of Innocence." Children from this era were innocent, she argues, because they were sheltered from "knowledge of the adult world." In an apparent attempt to equate television with the biblical tree of knowledge, she asserts that it is no longer possible to shelter children from adult knowledge:

> Television, virtually uncontrolled in all but a minority of homes, has caused children to gorge on the fruit of knowledge, not only about sex but also about the complexities of life in general. . . . Children are absorbing new information, and that touching trust once synonymous with childhood fades into premature skepticism and uncertainty.[6]

While Winn feels that television is largely to blame for the erosion of childhood innocence, she does not completely absolve parents. In her opinion, recent changes in parental attitudes have increased television's corruptive power. She emphasizes this point in her 1983 article, "The Loss of Childhood," as well as in her book *Children Without Childhood*. She claims that in the past parents felt obligated to protect their children from the realities of the adult world, but this feeling has given way to a belief that "children must be exposed early to adult experience in order to survive in an increasingly uncontrollable world."[7] As Winn sees it, this new attitude has led parents not to place restrictions on what their children watch on television, and this has caused children's lives to "become more difficult, more confusing—in short, more like adult lives."[8]

Winn also condemns parents for relying on television to achieve domestic tranquility. She feels that television is too often used to pacify children while their parents prepare dinner or engage in some other adult-centered activity. This tactic, she says, has taken the place of parental discipline, which in turn has undermined parental authority:

> Instead of having to establish rules and limits, an arduous and often frustrating job, instead of having to work at socializing children in order to make them more agreeable to live with, parents could solve all of their problems by resorting to the television set. . . .
>
> Television brought peace—but at a price. Without establishing firm rules and precise boundaries, parents never defined for the children precisely what the roles of the adults and the children in the family were to be. And without having to take an authoritative position right from the start, parents never gained the control of their children that their counterparts of the past achieved quite inevitably, out of sheer necessity. A new equality between adults and children became possible.[9]

In *The Hurried Child*, David Elkind makes many of the same points that Winn makes in her writings. He does, however, come up with an additional argument against television. He focuses his argument on the commercials that accompany Saturday morning cartoons and other children's programs. As Elkind points out, advertisers spend over $600 million a year to produce and air commercials that are aimed at children. Advertisers do this in the hope that the children who view the commercials will convince their parents to buy the advertised products. Elkind feels that this type of advertising helps diminish the differences between children and adults. "Television," he writes, "hurries children by treating them as consumers, as if they were adult wage earners with the capacity to see through the deceptions of advertising."[10]

Of the three critics, Neil Postman is the most strident. As he sees it, television is not only an important factor in the blurring of the line between childhood and adulthood; it is the only significant factor. Postman argues that the idea that children are different from adults is a direct result of the invention of the printing press. In Postman's opinion, the advent of printing elevated the importance of reading, and since reading is a difficult skill to acquire it became necessary to teach it to children. Thus, according to Postman, children started to be sent to schools, resulting in the segregation of children from adults. Postman concludes his tidy scenario by arguing that once this segregation process was underway adults began withholding certain types of information from children. Adults were able to do this, Postman claims, by confining the "secret" information to books and other publications that children were either incapable of or prohibited from reading. Postman maintains that this enforced ignorance made childhood innocence possible.[11]

In the second half of his book, Postman argues that television has replaced the print media as the primary avenue by which people make connections with the outside world. This development, he asserts, has erased the "dividing line between childhood and adulthood," for unlike the print media, television "requires no instruction to grasp its form."[12] Postman feels that because children can comprehend most television programs, it is now much more difficult for adults to keep secrets from children. He specifically refers to the "adult secrets" of sex and violence, subjects which he feels children should not know very much about until they reach adulthood. As he puts it, "in having access to the previously hidden fruit of adult information," contemporary children "are expelled from the garden of childhood."[13]

Postman is well aware that his views on childhood are quite similar to the views expressed by much of the New Right, and he feels somewhat defensive about this similarity. He takes pains to distance himself from the New Right's political agenda and accuses them of engaging in "religious bigotry." He does, however, praise their attempts to shelter children from "the new information environment," even though he feels that these attempts will ultimately fail.[14] He also feels that the New Right is to be admired for leading the attack against modern child-rearing beliefs and practices:

> The liberal tradition has tended to encourage the decline of childhood by its generous acceptance of all that is modern, and a corresponding hostility to anything that tries to "turn back the clock." But in some respects the clock is wrong, and the Moral Majority may serve as a reminder of a world that was once hospitable to children and felt deeply responsible for what they might become. It is permissible, I think, for those of us who disapprove of the arrogance of the Moral Majority to borrow some of their memories.[15]

In borrowing the New Right's idealization of childhood, Winn, Elkind, and Postman make the same mistake that those on the New Right make when they talk about the history of childhood; that is, they assume that the children from the preceding generation really were paragons of innocence. This is nothing new. Anthony Comstock made precisely the same assumption when he argued that the children of the 1880s were no longer innocent because they were reading dime novels. The problem with this line of reasoning is that it presupposes that childhood innocence is something more than a cultural ideal. Since Comstock's time, every generation of adults has had difficulty reconciling this ideal with the behavior of real children. Some adults, of course, recognized it as an ideal and did not become alarmed when their children failed to measure up to it. Others, though, became distressed when they discovered that their children were behaving in ways that did not seem especially innocent, and they came to the conclusion that something had gone terribly wrong with the younger generation. Invariably, that something was an aspect of American culture that made these adults uncomfortable. Whether it was dime novels, series books, radio programs, comic books, movies, rock 'n' roll, realistic novels, or textbooks, the argument was always the same—the cultural form was accused of destroying childhood innocence. Thus, the accusations that Winn, Elkind, and Postman make against television are simply the most recent manifestation of a century-old argument.

The points that these critics make in their books cannot be dismissed entirely. Television may have changed the lives of children, for example, and it is worth recognizing the possibility. So long as we are aware of their tendency to romanticize the past, we can use their writings to help us understand the impact of television on childhood. Also, their observation that childhood innocence is disappearing has some validity. As an idea, childhood innocence has its own history. It enjoyed widespread acceptance during the second half of the nineteenth century, but it has been gradually declining ever since Freud published his famous essay on infant sexuality in 1905. In contemporary America, most adults no longer ascribe to the idea of childhood innocence. This is a major development and one that warrants thought, which is, as Huck Finn said in a somewhat different context, interesting, but hard.

Notes

1. The Idea of Childhood Innocence and Its Impact on Children's Culture

1. Philip Greven, *The Protestant Temperament: Patterns of Child-Rearing, Religious Experience, and the Self in Early America* (New York: Alfred A. Knopf, 1977), 28–55. See also John Demos, *A Little Commonwealth: Family Life in Plymouth Colony* (New York: Oxford University Press, 1970), 131–40.
2. Cited in Zena Sutherland, Dianne L. Monson, and Mary Hill Arbuthnot, *Children and Books*, 6th ed. (Glenview, Ill.: Scott, Foresman and Co., 1981), 61.
3. Ibid., 60–61.
4. Greven, *The Protestant Temperament*, 269–81.
5. Ibid., 156–77.
6. C. John Sommerville, *The Rise and Fall of Childhood* (Beverly Hills, Cal.: Sage Publications, 1982), 121–24.
7. Samuel F. Pickering, Jr., *John Locke and Children's Books in Eighteenth-Century England* (Knoxville, Tenn.: University of Tennessee Press, 1981), 13–16.
8. Rosalie V. Halsey, *Forgotten Books of the American Nursery: A History of the Development of the American Story Book* (Boston: Charles E. Goodspeed and Co., 1911), 102–7.

9. Jacqueline S. Reinier, "Rearing the Republican Child: Attitudes and Practices in Post-Revolutionary Philadelphia," *William and Mary Quarterly*, 39, No. 1 (1982), 155.

10. L. Terry Oggel, "The Background of the Images of Childhood in American Literature," *Western Humanities Review*, 33, No. 4 (1979), 287–89.

11. Jean Jacques Rousseau, *Emile*, trans. Barbara Foxley (London: J. M. Dent & Sons, 1974), 56.

12. Bernard Wishy, *The Child and the Republic: The Dawn of Modern American Child Nurture* (Philadelphia: University of Pennsylvania Press, 1968), 21–23, 42–49. See also David J. Pivar, *Purity Crusade: Sexual Morality and Social Control, 1869–1900* (Westport, Conn.: Greenwood Press, 1973), 80–81.

13. Cited in Wishy, *The Child and the Republic*, 23.

14. For additional information on American children's literature from this period see Alice M. Jordan, *From Rollo to Tom Sawyer and Other Papers* (Boston: Horn Book, Inc., 1948); Anne Scott Macleod, *A Moral Tale: Children's Fiction and American Culture, 1820–1860* (Hamden, Conn.: Archon Books, 1975).

15. Jacob Abbott, *Rollo at Play* (New York: Thomas Y. Crowell and Co., 1897, first ed., 1838), 3.

16. John B. Crume, "Children's Magazines, 1826–1857," *Journal of Popular Culture*, 6, No. 4 (1973), 698–705.

17. "Prospectus of Youth's Companion," in *Youth's Companion*, ed. Lovell Thompson (Cambridge, Massachusetts: Houghton Mifflin Co., 1954), 1124.

18. David Wallace Adams and Victor Edmonds, "Making Your Move: The Educational Significance of the American Board Game, 1832 to 1904," *History of Education Quarterly*, 17, No. 4 (1977), 368.

19. Ibid., 370.

20. Wishy, *The Child and the Republic*, 94–104.

21. Ruby Takanishi, "Childhood as a Social Issue: Historical Roots of Contemporary Child Advocacy Movements," *Journal of Social Issues*, 34, No. 2 (1978), 11–16.

22. Jordan, *From Rollo to Tom Sawyer*, 33–39.

2. Anthony Comstock's Crusade Against Dime Novels

1. Throughout this work I will refer to half-dime novels, story papers, and boys' papers as dime novels.

2. W.H. Bishop, "Story-Paper Literature," *Atlantic Monthly*, September 1879, 385. For more background information on dime novels see Albert Johannsen, *The House of Beadle and Adams* (Norman, Okl.: University of Oklahoma Press, 1950); Daryl Jones, *The Dime Novel Western* (Bowling Green, Ohio: Popular Press, 1978); Edmund Pearson, *Dime Novels; or, Following an Old Trail in Popular Literature* (Boston: Little Brown and Co., 1929).

3. Heywood Broun and Margaret Leech, *Anthony Comstock: Roundsman of the Lord* (New York: Albert and Charles Boni, 1927), 56. See also Ralph K. Andrist, "Paladin of Purity," *American Heritage*, October 1973, 6.

4. Cited in Broun and Leech, *Anthony Comstock: Roundsman of the Lord*, 55–56.

5. For more information on Comstock's career see Broun and Leech, *Anthony Comstock: Roundsman of the Lord*; Charles Galluadet Trumbull, *Anthony Comstock, Fighter* (New York: Fleming H. Revell Co., 1913).

6. New York Society for the Suppression of Vice, *Fourth Annual Report* (New York, 1878), 7.

7. New York Society for the Suppression of Vice, *Sixth Annual Report* (New York, 1880), 6.

8. New York Society for the Suppression of Vice, *Eighth Annual Report* (New York, 1882), 7.

9. New York Society for the Suppression of Vice, *Sixth Annual Report*, 6.

10. Ibid., 7.

11. Ibid.

12. New York Society for the Suppression of Vice, *Ninth Annual Report* (New York, 1883), 9.

13. Ibid.

14. Anthony Comstock, *Traps for the Young* (New York: Funk and Wagnalls, 1883), 5.

15. Ibid., 25.

16. Ibid., 42.

17. New York Society for the Suppression of Vice, *Eighth Annual Report*, 9.

18. "Listening to Mr. Comstock," *New York Times*, 1 March 1882.

19. Cited in Paul S. Boyer, *Purity in Print: The Vice-Society*

Movement and Book Censorship in America (New York: Charles Scribner's Sons, 1968), 11.
20. Pivar, *Purity Crusade*, 184.
21. Comstock, *Traps for the Young*, 244.
22. Pivar, *Purity Crusade*, 184.
23. Comstock, *Traps for the Young*, 132.
24. Ibid., 133.
25. For a discussion of Comstock's tendency to project his own sexual feelings upon others see Harvey O'Higgins and Edward H. Reede, *The American Mind in Action* (New York: Harper and Brothers, 1924), 132–40.
26. Comstock, *Traps for the Young*, 239.
27. Ibid., 240.
28. Ibid., 240–41.
29. Ibid., 20.
30. Ibid., 21.

3. The Response of Children's Librarians to Dime Novels and Series Books

1. For more information on the relationship between professionalism and child-rearing see Christopher Lasch, *Haven in a Heartless World: The Family Besieged* (New York: Basic Books, 1977), 12–21.
2. Elizabeth Nesbitt, "Major Steps Forward," in *A Critical History of Children's Literature*, ed. Cornelia Miegs (New York: Macmillan Co., 1953), 416–24.
3. "Dime Novel Work," *Library Journal*, March-April 1883, 92.
4. W.H. Brett, "Books for Youth," *Library Journal*, June 1885, 128.
5. Jordan, *From Rollo to Tom Sawyer*, 34–55.
6. "Trashy and Vicious," *New York Times*, 19 March 1885.
7. "The Pawtucket Free Public Library and the Dime Novel," *Library Journal*, May 1885, 105.
8. Samuel S. Green, "Sensational Fiction in Public Libraries," *Library Journal*, September 1879, 348–49.
9. Ibid., 348.
10. Carolin M. Hewins, "Yearly Report on Boys' and Girls' Reading," *Library Journal*, July-August 1882, 185.
11. Ibid., 184.
12. Jordan, *From Rollo to Tom Sawyer*, 30.

13. For profiles of several of the earliest children's librarians see R. R. Bowker, "Some Children's Librarians," *Library Journal*, 1 October 1921, 787–90; R. R. Bowker, "Some More Children's Librarians," *Library Journal*, 1 May 1922, 393–96. Of the twenty-one librarians whom Bowker mentions, all were women and only two were married.
14. Martha H. Brooks, "Sunday School Libraries," *Library Journal*, April 1899, 149.
15. Clara W. Hunt, "Some Means by Which Children May Be Led to Read Better Books," *Library Journal*, April 1899, 149.
16. Henry L. Elmendorf, "Public Library Books in Public Schools," *Library Journal*, April 1900, 165.
17. Grace Thompson, "On the Selection of Books for Children," *Library Journal*, October 1907, 427.
18. E. F. Bleiler, "Introduction," in *Eight Dime Novels*, ed. E. F. Bleiler (New York: Dover Publications, Inc., 1974), ix.
19. For more information about girls' series books see Rebecca A. Freligh, "From Elsie Dinsmore to Nancy Drew: Girls' Series Books in American Culture," Ph. D. dissertation, Michigan State University, 1971.
20. Alice I. Hazeltine, "The Children's Librarian as a Book Buyer," *Library Journal*, 1 June 1923, 507.
21. Clara W. Hunt, "The Children's Library, a Moral Force," *Library Journal*, August 1906, 98.
22. Mary E. S. Root, "Time-Killers," *Wilson Bulletin*, June 1929, 675.
23. Adeline B. Zachert, "What Our Children Read and Why," *Library Journal*, January 1914, 23.
24. Caroline Burnite, "The Standard of Selection of Children's Books," *Library Journal*, April 1911, 164.
25. Ibid.
26. Mary E. S. Root, "Not to Be Circulated," *Wilson Bulletin*, January 1929, 446.
27. Ernest F. Ayres, "Not to Be Circulated," *Wilson Bulletin*, March 1929, 528.
28. Lillian Herron Mitchell, "Not to Be Circulated," *Wilson Bulletin*, April 1929, 580.
29. Ibid., 584.
30. Ibid., 580, 584.

4. Adult Reactions to Children's Radio Programs

1. For more background information about children's radio programs see Jim Harmon, *The Great Radio Heroes* (New York: Ace Books, Inc., 1967); Bruce Smith, *The History of Little Orphan Annie* (New York: Ballantine Books, 1982), 34–45; Robert West, *The Rape of Radio* (New York: Rodin Publishing Co., 1941), 148–61.
2. Daniel J. Boorstin, *The Americans: The Democratic Experience* (New York: Vintage Books, 1974), 230–37.
3. "Mothers Protest Bogyman on Radio," *New York Times*, 27 February 1933.
4. "Broadcasters Act to Curb Bogyman," *New York Times*, 28 February 1933.
5. Azriel L. Eisenberg, *Children and Radio Programs* (New York: Columbia University Press, 1936), 19.
6. Clara Savage Littledale, "Better Radio Programs for Children," *Parents' Magazine*, May 1933, 13.
7. Charles W. Whinston, Letter, *New York Times*, 12 March 1933.
8. Ludmila Jaffe, Letter, *New York Times*, 26 April 1935, 20.
9. Dorothy Gordon, *All Children Listen* (New York: George W. Stewart, 1942), 51–52.
10. Orrin E. Dunlap, "Higher Radio Standards," *New York Times*, 19 May 1935.
11. "Women's Radio Committee Discloses Its Formula for Approval of Children's Programs," *New York Times*, 29 December 1935.
12. For more information on the early history of the child study movement see Simon H. Tulchin, "History of the Child Study Movement," *Welfare Magazine*, May 1926, 12–25.
13. "Parents Are Wondering," *New York Times*, 25 November 1934.
14. "Mothers Give Skit to Test Radio Aims," *New York Times*, 20 February 1935.
15. Gordon, *All Children Listen*, 45.
16. "Scarsdale Mothers Debate Broadcasts," *New York Times*, 21 February 1935, 10.
17. "Children's Programs by the Columbia Broadcasting Company," *School and Society*, 25 May 1935, 700–1.

18. "Air Reform Praised by U.S. Radio Head," *New York Times*, 16 May 1935, 5.
19. "Curb on Radio Ads Pleases Stations," *New York Times*, 15 May 1935.
20. Orrin E. Dunlap, "Broadcasters Aim to Preserve Freedom of Speech," *New York Times*, 2 June 1935.
21. "Radio Gore Criticized for Making Children's Hour a Pause That Depresses," *Newsweek*, 8 November 1937, 26.
22. Gordon, *All Children Listen*, 58–59.
23. "Rates NBC Costs at $1,000,000,000," *New York Times*, 18 November 1938.
24. "Radio Denounced as Peril to Young," *New York Times*, 31 March 1938.
25. John J. DeBoer, "Radio: Pied Piper or Educator?" *Childhood Education*, October 1939, 76.
26. John J. DeBoer, "Radio and Children's Emotions," *School and Society*, 16 September 1939, 370.
27. Mary I. Preston, "Children's Reactions to Movie Horrors and Radio Crime," *Journal of Pediatrics*, 19, No. 2 (1941), 158.
28. "Crime Broadcasts Assailed by Panken," *New York Times*, 3 April 1938.
29. "Child Classic Program Competition for Thrillers," *Newsweek*, 19 December 1938, 32–34.
30. Maude Dunlop, "Radio Attuned to Young Ears," *New York Times*, 16 July 1939.
31. Gordon, *All Children Listen*, 54–57.
32. "Broadcasting Code Cuts Controversy," *New York Times*, 12 July 1939.
33. "The New Code for the Broadcasting Industry," *New York Times*, 12 July 1939.
34. Gordon, *All Children Listen*, 69–71.
35. J. Fred MacDonald, *Don't Touch That Dial: Radio Programming in American Life, 1920–1960* (Chicago: Nelson-Hall, 1979), 68–69.
36. "The Children's Hour," *Time*, 24 March 1947, 63.

5. Fredric Wertham and the Comic Book Controversy

1. Ralph G. Martin, "Doctor's Dream in Harlem," *New Republic*, 3 June 1946, 800.

2. Fredric Wertham, "Freud Now," *Scientific American*, October 1949, 53–54.
3. Fredric Wertham, *Seduction of the Innocent* (New York: Rinehart and Co., 1954), 10–16.
4. Les Daniels, *Comix: A History of Comic Books in America* (New York: Bonanza Books, 1971), 9–17.
5. Fredric Wertham, "The Comics . . . Very Funny!" *Saturday Review of* Literature, 29 May 1948, 29.
6. Ibid., 28.
7. Ibid., 29.
8. Ibid., 29.
9. Ibid., 28.
10. "Juvenile Delinquency Seen on Increase," *New York Times*, 24 June 1948.
11. "Urges Comic Book Ban," *New York Times*, 4 September 1948.
12. Frederic M. Thrasher, "The Comics and Delinquency: Cause or Scapegoat," *Journal of Educational Sociology*, December 1949, 195.
13. "The Couch Cult," *Time*, 11 September 1950, 87.
14. Wertham, *Seduction of the Innocent*, 296–304.
15. "Psychiatrist Asks Crime Comics Ban," *New York Times*, 14 December 1950.
16. "Health Law Urged to Combat Comics," *New York Times*, 4 December 1951.
17. "Comic Book Curbs Voted in Assembly," *New York Times*, 13 March 1952.
18. "Comic Book Curb Vetoed by Dewey," *New York Times*, 15 April 1952.
19. Daniels, *Comix: A History of Comic Books in America*, 85.
20. Wertham, *Seduction of the Innocent*, 393.
21. Ibid., 116.
22. Ibid., 118.
23. Ibid., 191.
24. Ibid., 193.
25. Ibid., 396.
26. Ibid., 97–98.
27. Daniels, *Comix: A History of Comic Books in America*, 84.
28. Fredric Wertham, "Do the Crime Comic Books Promote

Juvenile Deliquency?" *Congressional Digest*, December 1954, 302.

29. Ibid., 304.
30. Horror Comics, *Time*, 3 May 1954, 78. See also "Are Comics Horrible?" *Newsweek*, 3 May 1954, 60.
31. "Comics Book Industry Organizes to Enforce Ethical Standards," *Library Journal*, 15 October 1954, 1968–69. See also "Horror on the Newstands," *Time*, 27 September 1954, 77.
32. Daniels, *Comix: A History of Comic Books in America*, 90.
33. Ibid., 84.
34. Fredric Wertham to Karl Menninger, 14 November 1955, Archives of The Menninger Foundation, Topeka, Kansas.
35. Reuben Fine, *A History of Psychoanalysis* (New York: Columbia University Press, 1979), 120–24.

6. Film Censorship, Sexuality, and the Youth of Kansas

1. Edward DeGrazia and Roger K. Newman, *Banned Films: Movies, Censors and the First Amendment* (New York: R. R. Bowker, 1982), 13–15.
2. Roscoe Born, "Move to Abolish Movie Censor Finis to Colorful Kansas Chapter," *Topeka Journal*, 7 March 1951.
3. Kansas State Board of Review, "Laws and Rules." 1917, Papers of the Kansas State Board of Review, Kansas State Historical Society, Topeka (hereafter cited as Board of Review MSS).
4. Kansas State Board of Review, "First Annual Report," 1918. Papers of Governor Arthur Capper, Kansas State Historical Society.
5. Ibid.
6. K. A. Harris, "Censorship in Kansas: A Dilemma," *Your Government: Bulletin of the Governmental Research Center*, 15 December, 1963, 1.
7. De Grazia and Newman, *Banned Films*, 25–35.
8. Isabel Obee to Roland E. Boyton, 21 February 1931, Board of Review MSS.
9. Kansas State Board of Review, "Minutes of Special Meeting," 28 April 1939, Board of Review, MSS.
10. Harris, "Censorship in Kansas," 1.
11. Born, "Move to Abolish Movie Censor."
12. De Grazia and Newman, *Banned Films*, 78–83.

13. Harold R. Fatzer to Francis Vaughn, 19 August 1952, Board of Review MSS.
14. Kansas State Board of Review, Card File, 1953, Board of Review MSS.
15. De Grazia and Newman, *Banned Films*, 86–87.
16. Frances Vaughn to Harold R. Fatzer, 7 July 1953, Board of Review MSS.
17. Harold R. Fatzer to Frances Vaughn, 10 July 1953, Board of Review MSS.
18. Arthur J. Stanley, Jr. to Frances Vaughn, 8 September 1953, Board of Review MSS.
19. Kansas State Board of Review, Card File, 1953, Board of Review MSS.
20. Arthur J. Stanley, Jr., "Brief of Defendants," July 1954, Board of Review MSS.
21. "Judge on Vacation, So Film 'Moon Is Blue' Still Banned," *Topeka Journal* 20 July 1954.
22. "Movie Censorship Repealed in Kansas, "*Topeka Capital*, 8 April 1955.
23. "High Court Upholds Ban on 'Moon,' " *Topeka Journal*, 9 April 1955.
24. "Law Abolishing Movie Censors Ruled Invalid," *Topeka Capital*, 18 June 1955.
25. "Movie Censorship Still in Force, Says Fatzer," *Topeka Capital*, 25 October 1955.
26. Ira H. Carmen, *Movies, Censorship, and the Law* (Ann Arbor, Mich.: University of Michigan Press, 1966), 64–65.
27. "Quits as Movie Censor," *Kansas City Times*, 19 January 1956.
28. "Review Board Members Give Case for Movie Censorship," *Topeka Capital*, 12 March 1957.
29. Mary Cook to Clark Kuppinger, 6 March 1957, Board of Review MSS.
30. Harris, "Censorship in Kansas," 2.
31. De Grazia and Newman, *Banned Films*, 228–29.
32. Ephraim S. London to Mary Cook, 23 December 1957, Board of Review MSS.
33. De Grazia and Newman, *Banned Films*, 96.
34. Mary Cook to Ephraim S. London, 2 January 1958, Board of Review MSS.

35. Mary Cook to August Lauterbac, 2 January 1958, Board of Review MSS.
36. Hazel Runyan to Harold H. Harding, 14 April 1958, Board of Review MSS.
37. Harold H. Harding to Hazel Runyan, 28 April 1958, Board of Review MSS.
38. O. Q. Claflin, II, "Journal Entry of Judgment," 5 March 1959, Board of Review MSS.
39. "State Film Censor Law Struck Down," *Topeka Journal*, 27 July 1966.
40. William H. Avery to Pauline Kirk, 1 August 1966, Board of Review MSS.

7. Elvis Presley, Jimmy Snow, and the Controversy Over Rock 'n' Roll

1. Martin, Linda and Kerry Segrave, *Anti-Rock: The Opposition to Rock 'n' Roll* (Hamden, Conn.: Archon Books, 1988).
2. Albert Goldman, *Elvis* (New York: Avon, 1982), 139–40.
3. Ibid., 184–85.
4. Ibid., 133.
5. Arnold Shaw, *The Rockin' '50s* (New York: Hawthorn Books, 1974), 154.
6. Jerry Hopkins, *Elvis: A Biography* (New York: Warner Books, 1972), 133.
7. Ibid.
8. Jack Gould, "TV: New Phenomenon," *New York Times*, 6 June 1956.
9. Jack Gould, "TV: Report on a Week-End's Viewing," *New York Times*, 10 September 1956.
10. Jack Gould, "Elvis Presley: Lack of Responsibility Is Shown by TV in Exploiting Teen-Agers," *New York Times*, 16 September 1956.
11. Hopkins, *Elvis*, 251.
12. Jimmy Snow, *I Cannot Go Back* (Plainfield, N. J.: Logos International, 1977), 10–11.
13. Goldman, *Elvis*, 183.
14. Snow, *I Cannot Go Back*, 40.
15. Ibid., 47.
16. Ibid., 5.
17. Ibid., 59–61.

18. Ibid., 73–74.
19. Ibid., 77.
20. Ibid., 78.
21. "Evangelist Says Rock 'n' Roll Cause of Much Delinquency." *Tennessean*, 20 February 1960.
22. "Evangelist Snow to Appear in TV Show on Presley", *Savannah Morning News*, 4 March 1960.
23. "One-Time Rock 'n' Roller Assailing Its Evil Ways." *Miami Herald*, 9 February 1963.
24. Bob Bell, Jr., "Faith, Prayer, Patience Formula for New Church." *Nashville Banner*, 3 April 1968.
25. Jack Hurst, "Reverend Snow and Johnny Cash Build a Temple," *Tennessean*, 28 May 1972.

8. The New Right Versus the New Realists

1. Kenneth L. Woodward, John Barnes, and Laurie Lisle, "Born Again: The Year of the Evangelicals," *Newsweek*, 25 October 1976, 66–78.
2. Anne Scott MacLeod, "An End to Innocence: The Transformation of Childhood in Twentieth-Century Children's Literature," in *Opening Texts: Psychoanalysis and the Culture of the Child*, ed. Joseph H. Smith and William Kerrigan (Baltimore: Johns Hopkins University Press, 1985), 100–17.
3. Betsy Lee, *Judy Blume's Story* (New York: Vagabond Books, 1981), and Norma Klein, *Something About the Author Autobiography Series*, vol. 1 (Detroit: Gale Research, 1985), 155–68.
4. Norma Klein, "What Is Fit for Children?" *New York Times Book Review*, 24 August 1986, 20.
5. Richard Jackson, interview with author, New York City, 14 June 1985.
6. Norma Klein, "Some Thoughts on Censorship," *Top of the News*, 32 (Winter 1983): 150.
7. Judy Blume, interview with author, New York City, 10 June 1985.
8. "Censorship Dateline," *Newsletter on Intellectual Freedom*, June 1974, 8.
9. "Censorship Dateline," *Newsletter on Intellectual Freedom*, June 1977, 99–100.

10. "Censorship Dateline," *Newsletter on Intellectual Freedom*, November 1977, 155.

11. "Censorship Dateline," *Newsletter on Intellectual Freedom*, January 1978, 7.

12. "Censorship Dateline," *Newsletter on Intellectual Freedom*, May 1978, 57.

13. "North Carolina Moral Majority Listing 'Harmful' School Books," *Newsletter on Intellectual Freedom*, July 1981, 85.

14. Judith M. Goldberger, "Judy Blume: Target of the Censor," *Newsletter on Intellectual Freedom*, May 1981, 61.

15. "Censorship Dateline," *Newsletter on Intellectual Freedom*, July 1980, 77. See also "Censorship Dateline," *Newsletter on Intellectual Freedom*, May 1981, 66–67.

16. "Banned Book Week," *Publishers Weekly*, 27 August 1982, 264.

17. "Censorship Dateline," *Newsletter on Intellectual Freedom*, January 1985, 8.

18. "Schools Remove Three Judy Blume Books," *Charlotte Observer*, 11 November 1984.

19. "Authors Protest Peoria Ban on Blume Books," *Publishers Weekly*, 7 December 1984, 21.

20. "A Split Decision: Judy Blume in Peoria," *Newsletter on Intellectual Freedom*, March 1985, 33.

21. "Censorship Dateline," *Newsletter on Intellectual Freedom*, March 1982, 43.

9. The Tennessee Textbook Controversy

1. Edward B. Jenkinson, "How the Mel Gablers Have Put Textbooks on Trial," in *Dealing with Censorship*, ed. James E. Davis (Urbana, Ill.: National Council of Teachers of English, 1979), 108–16.

2. David Bollier, *Liberty and Justice for Some* (New York: Frederick Ungar Publishing Co., 1982), 20.

3. Beth McLeod, "Are These Textbooks Wrong?" *Johnson City Press-Chronicle*, 27 November 1983.

4. Vicki Frost, "Deposition," January 1986. This deposition and other documents related to this case are housed in the offices of Wilmer, Cutler & Pickering, a law firm in Washington, D. C. Hereafter these papers will be cited as WC & P Files.

5. "Plaintiffs' Objections by Book," July 1986, WC & P Files.
6. Frost, "Deposition," January 1986, WC & P Files.
7. McLeod, "Are These Textbooks Wrong?"
8. Church Hill: The Scopes Trial of the 1980s," *The Vigil*, March 1986, 8.
9. Ibid.
10. Frost, "Deposition," January 1986, WC & P Files.
11. Jennie Wilson, "Deposition," December 1985, WC & P Files.
12. "Schools Sued over Secular Humanism," *NEA Today*, March 1986.
13. Robert Mozert, "Deposition," January 1986, WC & P Files.
14. "Plaintiffs' Objections by Book," July 1986, WC & P Files.
15. Melinda Beck, "A Reprise of Scopes," *Newsweek*, 28 July 1986, 18–20.
16. "Plaintiffs' Objections by Book," July 1986, WC & P Files.
17. David Brooks, "COBS Parents File Lawsuuit in Hawkins Textbook Dispute," *Kingsport Times-News*, 3 December 1983.
18. Ibid.
19. Ibid.
20. "Hawkins Dilemma: Residents Organize Fight Against Ultra-Conservatism," *TEA News*, 9 January 1984.
21. Janet Day, "Judge Dismisses Hawkins Text Lawsuit," *Kingsport Times-News*, 16 March 1984.
22. Tim Elledge, "Textbook Feud Splits Bible Belt Community," *Citizen Journal*, 12 September 1985.
23. Mike Dye, "D. C. Law Firm to Handle Brunt of Book Case," *Kingsport Times-News*, 13 July 1986.
24. Timothy B. Dyk, interview with author, Washington, D.C., 13 February 1987.
25. Cameron Judd, "Gabler: Grandfatherly Critic of Textbooks," *Greeneville Sun*, 18 July 1986.
26. Ron Schaming, "Textbook Case in Hands of Judge Hull," *Greeneville Sun*, 23 July 1986.
27. Thomas G. Hull, "Text of Hawkins County Textbook Decision," *Greeneville Sun*, 29 October 1986.
28. Joan Beck, "Greeneville Decision," *Charlotte Observer*, 24 December 1986.

29. "Decision in Church Hill," *Newsletter on Intelletual Freedom*, January 1987, 38.
30. Barbara Vobejda, "Fundamentalists Prevail on Texts," *Washington Post*, 25 October 1986.
31. Ibid.
32. Beck, "Greeneville Decision."
33. "Fundamentalists Win Ruling on Textbook," *Charlotte Observer*, 25 October 1986.
34. Timothy B. Dyk, "Brief of Appellants," Janaury 1987, WC & P Files.
35. Chief Judge Pierce Lively, "Opinion," August 1987, WC & P Files.

10. The Idealization of the Pretelevision Child

1. William Melody, *Children's Television: The Economics of Exploitation* (New Haven, Conn.: Yale University Press, 1973), 87.
2. Marie Winn, *The Plug-In Drug* (New York: Viking Press, 1977; New York: Bantam Book, 1978), 13–18.
3. Ibid., 139–40.
4. Ibid., 141.
5. Ibid., 142–45.
6. Marie Winn, "What Becomes of Childhood Innocence?" *New York Times Magazine*, 25 January 1981, 15–16.
7. Marie Winn, "The Loss of Childhood," *New York Times Magazine*, 8 May 1983, 18.
8. Ibid.
9. Marie Winn, *Children Without Childhood* (New York: Pantheon Books, 1983), 45–46.
10. David Elkind, *The Hurried Child: Growing Up Too Fast Too Soon* (Reading, Mass.: Addison-Wesley, 1981), 79.
11. Neil Postman, *The Disappearance of Childhood* (New York: Delacorte Press, 1982), 36–51.
12. Ibid., 80.
13. Ibid., 97.
14. Ibid., 148.
15. Ibid.

Bibliography

Abbott, Jacob. *Rollo at Play*. New York: Thomas Y. Crowell and Co., 1897.

Adams, David Wallace, and Victor Edmunds. "Making Your Move: The Educational Significance of the American Board Game." *History of Education Quarterly*, 17, No. 4 (1977): 359–83.

Andrist, Ralph K. "Paladin of Purity." *American Heritage*, October 1973.

Ayres, Ernest F. "Not to Be Circulated?" *Wilson Bulletin*, March 1929, 528–29.

Beck, Melinda. "A Reprise of Scopes." *Newsweek*, 28 July 1986, 18–20.

Bishop, W. H. "Story-Paper Literature." *Atlantic Monthly*, September 1879, 383–93.

Bleiler, E. F., ed. *Eight Dime Novels*. New York: Dover Publications, Inc., 1974.

Bollier, David. *Liberty and Justice for Some*. New York: Frederick Ungar Publishing Co., 1982.

Boorstin, Daniel J. *The Americans: The Democratic Experience*. New York: Vintage Books, 1974.

Bowker, R. R. "Some Children's Librarians." *Library Journal*, 1 October 1921, 787–90.

———. "Some More Children's Librarians." *Library Journal*, 1 May 1922, 393–96.

Boyer, Paul S. *Purity in Print: The Vice-Society Movement and Book Censorship in America.* New York: Charles Scribner's Sons, 1968.

Brett, W. H. "Books for Youth." *Library Journal*, June 1885, 127–28.

Brooks, Martha H. "Sunday School Libraries." *Library Journal*, April 1899, 338–41.

Broun, Heywood, and Margaret Leech. *Anthony Comstock: Roundsman of the Lord.* New York: Albert and Charles Boni, 1927.

Burnite, Caroline. "The Standard of Selection of Children's Books." *Library Journal*, April 1911, 161–66.

Carmen, Ira H. *Movies, Censorship and the Law.* Ann Arbor, Mich.: University of Michigan Press, 1966.

Comstock, Anthony, *Traps for the Young.* New York: Funk and Wagnalls, 1883.

Crume, John B. "Children's Magazines, 1826–1857." *Journal of Popular Culture* 6, No. 4 (1973): 698–706.

Daniels, Les. *Comix: A History of Comic Books in America.* New York: Bonanza Books, 1971.

DeBoer, John J. "Radio and Children's Emotions." *School and Society*, 16 September 1939, 369–73.

———."Radio: Pied Piper or Educator?" *Childhood Education*, October 1939, 74–79.

DeGrazia, Edward, and Roger K. Newman. *Banned Films: Movies, Censors and the First Amendment.* New York: R. R. Bowker, 1982.

Demos, John. *A Little Commonwealth: Family Life in Plymouth Colony.* New York: Oxford University Press, 1970.

Eisenberg, Azriel L. *Children and Radio Programs.* New York: Columbia University Press, 1936.

Elkind, David. *The Hurried Child: Growing Up Too Fast Too Soon.* Reading, Mass.: Addison-Wesley, 1981.

Elmendorf, Henry L. "Public Library Books in Public Schools." *Library Journal*, October 1907, 163–65.

Fine, Reuben. *A History of Psychoanalysis.* New York: Columbia University Press, 1979.

Freligh, Rebecca A. "From Elsie Dinsmore to Nancy Drew: Girls' Series Books in American Culture." Ph.D. dissertation Michigan State University, 1971.

Goldberger, Judith M. "Judy Blume: Target of the Censor." *Newsletter on Intellectual Freedom*, May 1981.

Goldman, Albert. *Elvis*. New York: Avon, 1982.

Gordon, Dorothy. *All Children Listen*. New York: George W. Stewart, 1942.

Green, Samuel S. "Sensational Fiction in Public Libraries." *Library Journal*, 1879, 345–55.

Greven, Philip. *The Protestant Temperament: Patterns of Child-Rearing, Religious Experience, and the Self in Early America*. New York: Alfred A. Knopf, 1977.

Halsey, Rosalie V. *Forgotten Books of the American Nursery: A History of the Development of the American Story-Book*. Boston: Charles E. Goodspeed and Co., 1911.

Harmon, Jim. *The Great Radio Heroes*. New York: Ace Books, Inc., 1967.

Hazeltine, Alice I. "The Children's Librarian as a Book Buyer." *Library Journal*, 1 June 1923, 505–9.

Hewins, Carolin M. "Yearly Report on Boys' and Girls' Reading." *Library Journal*, July-August 1882, 182–90.

Hopkins, Jerry. *Elvis: A Biography*. New York: Warner Books, 1972.

Hunt, Clara W. "The Children's Library, a Moral Force." *Library Journal*, August 1906, 97–103.

———. "Some Means by Which Children May Be Led to Read Better Books." *Library Journal*, April 1899, 147–49.

Jenkinson, Edward B. "How the Mel Gablers Have Put Textbooks on Trial." In *Dealing with Censorship*, edited by James E. Davis. Urbana, Ill.: National Council of Teachers of English, 1979.

Johannsen, Albert. *The House of Beadle and Adams*. Norman, Okla.: University of Oklahoma Press, 1950.

Jones, Daryl. *The Dime Novel Western*. Bowling Green, Ohio: Popular Press, 1978.

Jordan, Alice M. *From Rollo to Tom Sawyer and Other Papers*. Boston: Horn Book, Inc., 1948.

Klein, Norma. "Some Thoughts on Censorship." *Top of the News* 32, No. 2 (1983): 137–53.

———. "What Is Fit for Children?" *New York Times Book Review*, 24 August 1986, 20.

Lasch, Christopher. *Haven in a Heartless World: The Family Besieged*. New York: Basic Books, 1977.

Lee, Betsy. *Judy Blume's Story*. New York: Vagabond Books, 1981.

Littledale, Clara Savage. "Better Radio Programs for Children." *Parents' Magazine*, May 1933, 13.

MacDonald, J. Fred. *Don't Touch That Dial: Radio Programming in American Life, 1920–1960*. Chicago: Nelson-Hall, 1979.

MacLeod, Anne Scott. "An End to Innocence: The Transformation of Childhood in Twentieth-Century Children's Literature." In *Opening Texts: Psychoanalysis and the Culture of the Child*, edited by Joseph H. Smith and William Kerrigan. Baltimore: Johns Hopkins Univesity Press, 1985.

———. *A Moral Tale: Children's Fiction and American Culture, 1820–1860*. Hamden, Conn.: Archon Books, 1975.

Martin, Linda and Kerry Segrave. *Anti Rock: The Opposition to Rock 'n' Roll* Hamden, Conn.: Archon Books, 1988.

Martin, Ralph G. "Doctor's Dream in Harlem." *New Republic*, 3 June 1946, 798–800.

Meigs, Cornelia, ed. *A Critical History of Children's Literature*. New York: MacMillan Co., 1953.

Melody, William. *Children's Television: The Economics of Exploitation*. New Haven, Conn.: Yale University Press, 1973.

Mitchell, Lillian Herron. "Not to Be Circulated." *Wilson Bulletin*, April 1929.

Oggel, L. Terry. "The Background Images of Childhood in American Literature." *Western Humanities Review* 33, No. 4 (1979): 281–97.

O'Higgins, Harvey, and Edward H. Reede. *The American Mind in Action*. New York: Harper and Brothers, 1924.

Pearson, Edmund. *Dime Novels; or, Following an Old Trail in Popular Literature*. Boston: Little Brown and Co., 1929.

Pickering, Samuel F. *John Locke and Children's Books in Eighteenth-Century England*. Knoxville, Tenn.: University of Tennessee Press, 1981.

Pivar, David J. *Purity Crusade: Sexual Morality and Social Control, 1868–1900*. Westport, Conn.: Greenwood Press, Inc., 1973.

Postman, Neil. *The Disappearance of Childhood*. New York: Delacorte Press, 1982.

Preston, Mary I. "Children's Reactions to Movie Horrors and Radio Crime." *Journal of Pediatrics* 19, No. 2 (1941): 147–68.

Reinier, Jacqueline S. "Rearing the Republican Child: Attitudes and Practices in Post-Revolutionary Philadelphia." *William and Mary Quarterly* 39, No. 1 (1982): 150–63.

Root, Mary E. S. "Not to Be Circulated." *Wilson Bulletin*, January 1929, 446.

———. "Time-Killers." *Wilson Bulletin*, June 1929, 675–77.

Rousseau, Jean-Jacques. *Emile*. Trans. Barbara Foxley. London: J. M. Dent & Sons, 1974.

Shaw, Arnold. *The Rockin' '50s*. New York: Hawthorn Books, 1974.

Slater, Peter Gregg. *Children in the New England Mind: In Death and in Life*. Hamden, Conn.: Archon Books, 1977.

Smith, Bruce. *The History of Little Orphan Annie*. New York: Ballantine Books, 1982.

Snow, Jimmy. *I Cannot Go Back*. Plainfield, N.J.: Logos International, 1977.

Sommerville, C. John. *The Rise and Fall of Childhood*. Beverly Hills, Cal.: Sage Publications, 1982.

Sutherland, Zena, Dianne L. Monson, and Mary Hill Arbuthnot. *Children and Books*. 6th Ed. Glenview, Ill.: Scott, Foresman and Co., 1981.

Takanishi, Ruby. "Childhood as a Social Issue: Historical Roots of Contemporary Child Advocacy Movements." *Journal of Social Issues* 34, No. 2 (1978): 8–28.

Thompson, Grace. "On the Selection of Books for Children." *Library Journal*, October 1907, 427–31.

Thompson, Lovell, ed. *Youth's Companion*. Cambridge, Mass.: Houghton Mifflin Co., 1954.

Thrasher, Frederic M. "The Comics and Delinquency: Cause or Scapegoat." *Journal of Educational Sociology* 23, No. 4 (1949): 195–205.

Trumbull, Charles Gallaudet. *Anthony Comstock, Fighter*. New York: Fleming H. Revell Co., 1913.

Tulchin, Simon H. "A History of the Child Study Movement." *Welfare Magazine*, May 1926, 12–25.

Wertham, Fredric. "The Comics . . . Very Funny!" *Saturday Review of Literature*. 29 May 1948.

———. "Do the Crime Comic Books Promote Juvenile Delinquency?'' *Congressional Digest*, December 1954, 302–10.

———. ''Freud Now.'' *Scientific American*, October 1949, 50–54.

———. *Seduction of the Innocent*. New York: Rinehart and Co., 1954.

West, Robert. *The Rape of Radio*. New York: Rodin Publishing Co., 1941.

Winn, Marie. *Children Without Childhood*. New York: Pantheon Books, 1983.

———. ''The Loss of Childhood.'' *New York Times Magazine*, 8 May 1983, 18–30.

———. *The Plug-In Drug*. New York: Viking Press, 1977.

———. ''What Became of Childhood Innocence?'' *New York Times Magazine*, 25 January 1981.

Wishy, Bernard. *The Child and the Republic: The Dawn of Modern American Child Nurture*. Philadelphia: University of Pennsylvania Press, 1968.

Woodward, Kenneth L., John Barnes, and Laurie Lisle. ''Born Again: The Year of the Evangelicals.'' *Newsweek*, 25 October 1976, 68–78.

Zachert, Adeline B. ''What Our Children Read and Why.'' *Library Journal*, January 1914, 21–24.

Index